STO

ACPL ITEM
DISCARDED

3 1833 00303 3930

Y0-ACF-394

4-18-55

AMERICA'S ROLE IN
INTERNATIONAL
SOCIAL WELFARE

THE FLORINA LASKER LECTURES
DELIVERED AT COLUMBIA UNIVERSITY
UNDER THE SPONSORSHIP OF
THE NEW YORK SCHOOL OF SOCIAL WORK
MARCH AND APRIL, 1953

AMERICA'S ROLE IN INTERNATIONAL SOCIAL WELFARE

By ALVA MYRDAL

ARTHUR J. ALTMEYER

and DEAN RUSK

1955

COLUMBIA UNIVERSITY PRESS, NEW YORK

COPYRIGHT 1955
COLUMBIA UNIVERSITY PRESS
NEW YORK

PUBLISHED IN
GREAT BRITAIN, CANADA, INDIA, AND PAKISTAN
BY GEOFFREY CUMBERLEGE
OXFORD UNIVERSITY PRESS
LONDON, TORONTO, BOMBAY, AND KARACHI

MANUFACTURED IN THE
UNITED STATES OF AMERICA

LIBRARY OF CONGRESS CATALOG
CARD NUMBER: 54-12723

FLORINA LASKER

1884–1949

889904

THE FLORINA LASKER LECTURES were established with funds
from the Estate of Florina Lasker, a distinguished alumna of
the New York School of Social Work, who died in 1949. Born
in Galveston, Texas, Miss Lasker attended the University of
Texas and in 1915 came to New York for graduate study in social work. Thereafter she was prominently associated with various reform and welfare activities in that city. After completing
her studies she was associated with the Industrial Division of
the Russell Sage Foundation for several years. Following her
employment there, she became a volunteer worker for the
Bureau of Philanthropic Research and prepared an important
report on the Jewish blind in New York City. In 1934 she became Secretary of the New York Labor Study Commission.

She was long associated with the Consumers League of New
York, which she helped to reorganize in 1943 and of which
she served as President until shortly before her death. Under
her active leadership and with her financial assistance, the
League made a series of studies of the conditions of migrants
in New York State, studies which stimulated important legislative and administrative reforms. Miss Lasker was also prominent in the work of the National Consumers League. Along

with labor problems, she was deeply concerned with civil liberties and was a member of the Board of the American Civil Liberties Union for over twenty years, serving as the first Chairman of the New York Committee of the Union from its inception in 1932. For many years she was a member of the Board of the National Committee of Jewish Women, devoting her activities especially to problems of new immigrants to the United States.

The impact of Florina Lasker's vigorous and generous personality was especially valuable to the many agencies in New York with which she was associated in a voluntary capacity over three decades. In addition to financial support she gave freely of her own time and energy to them, and brought to bear on their problems and the formulation of their policies an incisive intelligence and a well-trained mind.

CONTENTS

INTRODUCTION

Selection of the topic "America's Role in International Social Welfare" as the focus of the second series of Florina Lasker Lectures needs little justification. During the last twenty years, and notably since the end of World War II, there has been a ferment at work throughout the world directed toward raising the living standards of people everywhere. It has been characterized not merely by concrete efforts to increase productivity in those countries that, significantly, we have come to call the "underdeveloped countries," but also by a determination that the benefits of higher output should be shared by all citizens and that the human costs of industrialization and the introduction of modern productive techniques should be minimized.

America has been deeply involved in these developments. Perhaps our greatest single contribution has been the diffusion of the idea that poverty is not inevitable: that higher standards of living are both possible and desirable and that man himself can in large measure control his economic destiny. In this sense, the mere existence of the high American standard of living has been a potent stimulant to change elsewhere. In fact, our influence has been much greater than this. We have played an active role, through the grant of material aid and training facilities and the services of expert personnel, in helping to bring about social and economic change in other countries.

Our involvement has stemmed from several causes. Ameri-

cans, cynical views to the contrary notwithstanding, are a generous and warmhearted people, and part of our involvement is
a purely disinterested desire to help others less fortunate than
we. In part, we are exerting an influence merely by reason of
the relative wealth of our resources and know-how. Other countries request us to send them experts and consultants, and foreign students come here for training. While much of this
dissemination of knowledge and techniques has been part of
a deliberately planned international aid program, some of it
would have occurred under any circumstances. Finally, we are
increasingly coming to recognize the close relationship between
low standards of living and the pressure for political change. In
the context of a world in which two conflicting political ideolo-
gies are struggling for the allegiance of men's minds, social
welfare has inevitably become an important component of foreign policy. Democracy, to win this battle, must be able to
demonstrate that it is both as concerned with, and as effective
as totalitarianism claims to be in doing something about the
shocking poverty which is still the lot of far too large a proportion of the human race.

Whatever its cause, our involvement in international social
welfare raises some major problems. The planned and conscious
efforts now being made in many countries to raise standards
of living and increase social welfare presuppose that the planners have clearly defined objectives, scientific methods of ana-
lyzing the causes of the evils to be remedied, and full awareness
of available techniques and programs and of their potentialities.
The efforts presuppose, in other words, that there is a science
of international social welfare. Lacking this, there can be no
guarantee that our policies will be well coordinated, that first
things will be put first, and that scarce resources will be used
with maximum effectiveness.

Since we are in fact influencing social policy and administration in other countries by sending American experts and consultants abroad and by serving as a major training center for foreign personnel, it is important to know whether the kind of training given in America is in fact appropriate to the needs and institutions of other countries. How far is American social work a uniquely American phenomenon? How much of American theory and professional skill is in fact exportable? How far do we, and can we, equip foreign personnel to contribute fruitfully to the solution of the social problems posed by their own countries?

These are challenging questions for those who are concerned with the development of sound social welfare policies or who are responsible for the training of social welfare personnel, and the three papers in this volume mirror this concern. The paper by Dr. Alva Myrdal, Director of the Department of Social Science, UNESCO, and formerly Top Ranking Director of Social Affairs, United Nations, explores the many challenging problems encountered in the effort to develop international social welfare activities on a sound, scientific basis. Mr. Arthur J. Altmeyer, who as Commissioner for Social Security until 1954 was in charge of the observation programs of many foreign social welfare students and who in his own person and through his staff has been closely involved in international advisory services, takes up the question of the kind of training that would seem most appropriate for those undertaking international social welfare responsibilities. Mr. Dean Rusk, President of The Rockefeller Foundation and formerly Assistant Secretary of State, sets social welfare policy in the context of our wider international relations.

The New York School of Social Work wishes to express to the participants its appreciation of the contributions they have made in these papers. We are deeply indebted to Miss Loula Lasker and Mrs. Etta Rosensohn, the trustees of the Florina Lasker Estate, whose gift made possible this lecture series.

EVELINE M. BURNS
Chairman, Florina Lasker Lecture Committee

AMERICA'S ROLE IN

INTERNATIONAL

SOCIAL WELFARE

A SCIENTIFIC APPROACH TO
INTERNATIONAL WELFARE

A LIST OF MAIN PROBLEMS

THE TASK which is implicit in the very title of my paper—to internationalize social welfare—is one which no generation before ours has had to face. The plight of the hitherto less privileged nations is beginning to weigh heavily on our conscience. Today, when all the modern means of communication keep us supplied with an incessant, vivid flow of information, we can no longer ignore that plight, as our forefathers did. The moral climate of our time—despite its many failings and even streaks of cruelty—has changed, too, toward a greater concern for human welfare. Personal or even national profit is no longer professed as a supreme value. Self-interest, when mentioned at all in political rationalization, must be "enlightened" and should preferably be demonstrated as being identical with the interests of others.

Such is the dilemma of our time: both our knowledge of the evil that exists and our aspirations to overcome it have been raised to new heights. Although we cannot boast that welfare is the hallmark of our era, we are in quite a new degree concerned with the responsibility for it. This is true of countries as well as of individuals; welfare is claimed as the ultimate justification in the foreign policy of great nations and it is advertised as the real meaning of business. One's own profit and concern for others are thus intermingled in a way which indicates that "welfare" is now imposed upon us all as a supreme value and duty for national as well as international policy. Social workers in particular should be happy to note that to promote the public welfare, which has always been their professional ideal, is now becoming a definite commitment for ever widening circles of citizens, yes, of nations and their international agencies for cooperation. Cold-blooded exploitation, colonialism, or imperialism have become morally unacceptable.

While this consensus on objectives—or this moral pressure —is establishing itself more and more firmly in the Western countries, the "have-not" countries are beginning to discover their plight. They are just starting to make comparisons and to alert awakening millions of their citizens to the findings revealed. This pressure of public opinion from the underdeveloped countries works on the conscience of the Western world. The two phenomena—of increasing moral sensitivity on the part of the more privileged peoples and of growing impatience on the part of the others—are, of course, not disconnected. They strengthen each other. The psychic mechanism for making the self-interest of the "have" countries an enlightened one consists in a better understanding of the fact that the differing levels of welfare between countries create tensions that might one day become unmanageable. Particularly in this postwar period, with its mounting fear of war and its rising costs of defense, this dissatisfaction in hitherto underdeveloped nations is seen as a potential danger which cannot go unheeded.

To meet the very complex situation thus indicated, many countries in the Western world, and foremost among them the

United States, have launched a kind of modern crusade for helping the underdeveloped countries and endeavoring to raise them to a standard of living more commensurate with that of the rest of the world. Already the Charter of the United Nations pledged member states "to take joint and separate action . . . to promote higher standards of living, full employment and conditions of economic and social progress." The definite action taken so far has, we should stress, mostly the character of a spontaneous kind of aid in response to precipitous needs as they become internationally recognized. Faced with so tense a situation and being alive to the potential conflicts that result from inequality, the United Nations initiated action to promote development on a larger scale than ever envisaged before. So far, it has concentrated on sharing the technical know-how which has enriched the West. This action is in itself a tribute to mankind's most human qualities, and should never be belittled. But we must admit that it had never been the object of careful preparatory planning. A speech by President Truman in 1949, a vote by the Economic and Social Council of the United Nations, also in 1949, set in motion the international scheme known as Technical Assistance or the bilateral one known as the Point Four program. It can most appropriately be characterized as stemming from a combined drive of *humanitarian conscience* and *technocratic imagination,* both typical of our century. It is the specific effort of our time—and really the first effort of any time—toward international welfare.

But is it enough? Have we really faced the entire problem of international welfare? It is most important that we should be aware of the dramatic race being enacted beneath our eyes between our aid and the force of events: the gap is widening instead of closing, the poor countries are becoming poorer, the hungry continents are getting hungrier. Every year, when the Food and Agriculture Organization meets and reports, it calls attention to this most unfortunate trend. The dilemma is one between the slower increase in food production and the more rapid restoration of health. By thus reducing mortality and prolonging the period of life—"too fast" one is almost tempted to say—we make even more difficult the problem of maintaining the world's population on a decent level of consumption.

The food supplies per head for the world as a whole (the USSR excluded from the comparison) in 1948–50 were only 95 percent of prewar supplies.[1] This, in fact, gives too rosy a picture. Some increase of production had occurred during the period but only in those parts of the world which were already food surplus areas: the United States, Canada, Australia, New Zealand. In the remaining areas (again excluding the USSR), containing over 90 percent of the world population, agricultural production in the period 1948–50 averaged slightly below prewar output, with the result that supplies per head there averaged only 90 percent of the 1934–38 levels.

A main conclusion therefore immediately forces itself upon us: the pace of improvement is too slow. All the measures to step up the development process and increase welfare run the risk of appearing as palliatives in comparison with the ever growing needs. Thus the major question, which within the scope of this paper I cannot explore, but which we must always bear in mind, is that of the adequacy, on the whole, of the attempts at concerted international action hitherto undertaken. Are we fighting a losing battle, wherein Point Four and Techni-

[1] This and the following figures, emanating from the Food and Agriculture Organization, are quoted from F. L. McDougall, "Food and Population," *International Conciliation*, No. 486, December, 1952 (Carnegie Endowment for International Peace), which is the most conveniently available reference for American readers.

cal Assistance and all the other measures of which we are so proud are only rear-guard actions?

There is obviously need for a dispassionate scientific analysis in which the sum total of their effects on the relative economic well-being of countries would be established, including the matters I intend to exclude from the rest of my paper: what has happened to capital movements, to raw material prices, and to many other factors in the composite picture of world economy? It must be recognized that, despite laudable efforts to aid the underprivileged countries to develop, they seem to be the losers in the race between increasing productivity and the increase of population.

Restricting our attention to what happens directly to social welfare—measured as it should be in terms of consumption, longevity, social stability—what has been said should serve as a reminder of the dimensions which any welfare program must have if it is to call itself international. It would even have to close the gap between happy and unhappy regions which economic development seems to widen. Although nothing but a scientific approach could give us a definite measure of what is done or what needs to be done, I believe everybody agrees that what has been achieved so far has been too little and too late. And may I add that it takes courage which perhaps only science possesses to measure the full scope of existing and imminent world misery. My first entry on the list of soul-searching questions is therefore: have we mustered the courage and judged our international action to achieve universal welfare against the realistic background of immense and growing needs and cravings which exist, and against the population trends which threaten more desperate poverty?

If this sounds discouraging, it is only because of the aspirations we in the early civilized West are now professing. For if we measure instead against the deeds of earlier times, what is now being undertaken to improve welfare all over the world is truly gigantic. Space forbids an enumeration of all these activities, bilateral and international, for reconstruction, rehabilitation, and development aid which have marked the postwar period. As an indication, however, I might mention that the United Nations system alone, not counting the efforts of the United States, the Colombo Plan, or the inter-American activities, has during the last four years been sending out some 3,000 experts at the request of countries which consider themselves insufficiently developed.[2] The fellowships given to specialists in the underdeveloped countries for improving their knowledge by study abroad are many times greater.

My task, which is to project a scientific searchlight on to all these attempts, forces me to raise a second question: do the efforts so far undertaken aim as directly as they might toward increased social welfare, that is, human welfare? Are they not too optimistically directed toward an immediate increase of economic productivity, in the belief that such an increase would automatically ensure the welfare of the populations concerned? Are they not too little directed toward those factors which, in the special dynamics of any one country, could be considered as strategic for a long-term development that would both raise the level of production and of consumption and also assure the retention or recreation of indigenous values of culture and human rights?

There has been so far in all technical assistance attempts to

[2] A most convenient survey of the scope and structure of Technical Assistance has been made available to the interested public. See Walter Sharp, *International Technical Assistance* (Public Administration Service, Chicago, 1952).

improve international welfare a preponderant interest in *eco-nomic* development, symbolized by the very label chosen for concerted international action in this field—"Technical Assistance for Economic Development"—and borne out by the high numbers of engineers and other technicians concerned with production among the experts. The risk hereby encountered—and this stands out as the second large problem on the horizon of my topic—is that of *unbalanced development*. Certainly a scientific examination becomes urgent, as those whose vocation is social welfare must ask for an assessment of the total effects, disruptive as well as beneficial, of development measures undertaken so far.

This second question is intimately related to the ensuing general one, which a social scientist must put on the agenda, namely, to what extent is the internationally inspired attempt to step up action for social welfare part of integrated planning? Or, to put it more bluntly, to what extent is it uncoordinated, "spotty," *ad hoc* action—just doing good according to the principle that everything helps? If international action is of the latter type, it surely misses one of the most prominent features of our era. For the twentieth century is predominently an era of planning, taken in the widest sense of the word without implying planning of any specific political type. Even when it is a planning for retaining the *status quo*, planning it is. The attempt of laissez-faire liberalism to establish a sacred dogma against planning is dead; even the dialectics between planning and free enterprise, which filled the beginning of the century and, in particular, the inter-war period, have come to an end. No country has any scruples at all about matters like town and country planning. Most governments, no matter how loudly they might voice their hostility against planning, see themselves forced to introduce all kinds of controls, e.g., controls on prices. Public discussion now centers round the virtues and vices of specific controls rather than on the justification or not of planning.

Planning, i.e., conscious foresight as to the consequences and some subsequent adjustment of policy, is recognized as necessary. But it has to embrace both direct results and by-effects. It has now been generally recognized, with a sort of fatalism, that if we do not choose planning it will be forced upon us anyway. And it should be even more clear that the underdeveloped countries in particular do deliberately choose planning. They are impatient with the lag between their progress and that of other countries. They are determined to speed up history. I have just had an opportunity of observing the pride which countries like India and Egypt are taking in advertising their new plans. This is another of the new and characteristic features of our time, that governments shoulder a very much heavier responsibility than ever before for shaping the economic and social well-being of their populations.

Here we come to the crucial question: are the measures taken for the international promotion of welfare in keeping with such plans? This is not to be understood as any advocacy of planning by the international agencies. The plans must be, and are, the responsibility of the countries themselves, who alone can judge whether and how international measures fit into a long-range national plan.

The question, however, is a very wide one, and here I return to the particular topic of this paper: can truly coherent plans be established? Do we approach the problem scientifically? Have we the necessary scientific resources for it? And—even more specifically—how can we dare to suppose that the countries that are now only entering the path of development can master the *techniques for planning?* Here we meet a third general risk, namely, that measures taken remain well-meaning but *ad hoc* measures, and that perhaps what is the most urgent task of all, because it is primary to the others—to provide the resources of science and scientists for purposive, efficient national planning —remains neglected.

If these major risks enumerated so far are of a general kind, affecting any development process as such, there exists also a much more specific risk connected with the international efforts at aiding the new countries—the fourth on my list. This risk can briefly be described as that of development measures remaining *foreign*. And I do not merely mean unconnected with local conditions and directions of change, but exotic and strange in some of their features, introducing elements that run counter to certain indigenous values. To assert this is not to throw any major responsibility on the countries endeavoring to share their knowledge. In the case of the recipient countries also, it can be noted that measures have sometimes been welcomed because they have an attraction value as signs of "advancement," without a proper weighing of their intrinsic worth against those countries' own native cultures.

This general difficulty is evidently not so much of a risk in the purely technological domains. Natural science laws remain the same everywhere, the calculation of the tensility of a 12-mm. iron bar presumably being constant. But such is, as we well know, not the case in the economic and social fields. Nor even in the technological field can we altogether disregard the human factors. Thus it has been found that boot and shoe machinery, which is rented out by large international firms, has to be geared to a different psychomotor reaction speed according to the region in which it is to be used. If this adaptation of the mechanical rhythm to the human factor is not made when the machinery travels from Great Britain to Africa, penalties will have to be paid, perhaps in the breakdown of otherwise perfect machinery which will not serve its purpose of yielding the required production. Similarly, it is beginning to be recognized that agricultural implements for India might more appropriately be copied from Japan than from the West. In social welfare the risk of advice remaining foreign is blatantly visible. I need only point to the incompatibility, e.g., of advice from an American expert on introducing community chests and advice from a New Zealand expert on setting up a system of comprehensive social security.

Whatever the value of the examples, which can be multiplied by anybody who has looked over the scene in an underdeveloped country, the fact is that to a very large extent Technical Assistance as it has had to function in its first, experimental period has meant that underdeveloped countries become submitted to attempts to introduce one foreign element here, another there. The value of the attempts has been safeguarded by the common sense of experts and national agencies alike. But no international body has been taking the much greater trouble of efficiently harmonizing them or studying to what extent technical know-how in the social welfare field is exportable or importable at all.

In one way, what has been set out above as a list of main developmental risks is nothing but a reminder of the problem—so often raised rhetorically—of whether countries now setting out on the route to economic development and social welfare can avoid having to repeat the long history of the trials and tribulations of the Western world. Our history of industrialization is nothing but a giant record of a trial-and-error process. Ought not this experience to be put to use for the benefit of newcomers? I am, however, anxious not merely to repeat the general appeal, which has so often been made, but, alas, so far in vain, for a purposive search for the lessons history might have to teach in order to shorten the development process and take the worst edge off the adjustment hardships entailed. There are now so many new factors at play that history cannot be imitated, even if we so wished, nor are its lessons to be read off mechanically. Rather, history should be submitted to a theoretical scrutiny, comparing what would happen to one variable after another submitted to change, under different settings. Such a theoretical scrutiny of what can and what cannot be done in the social welfare field is what I am asking for.

Is it not possible to find certain identifiable aspects of the institutional and cultural life of each country which could offer criteria for judging the adequacy and appropriateness of measures envisaged for improving welfare? Has science no more powerful aid to give than that given so far? Cannot the collected experience of all the countries that have gone through more or less painful, more or less successful, developments toward welfare help? Cannot the systematic analysis of these experiences and of all the knowledge about countries and peoples which is assembled by the social sciences give more definite guidance? Cannot human brain power come to the rescue?

Welfare work and welfare workers must become science-minded as well as being humanitarian and full of practical ingenuity—two forces which have, we must admit, already carried the world greatly forward.

We might recall that the heyday of scientific optimism goes back to some hundred years ago; the early advances in the natural sciences led to the elaboration of lofty utopias, quite technocratic in their belief in the perfection of human social life. These advances in the natural sciences continued; they became more and more gigantic and came to reshape Western civilization. By the 1930's this rapid development had aroused some apprehension on the part of many observers of the changing cultures, from Oswald Spengler to Aldous Huxley. The latter may be said to have succeeded in bringing to the notice of the man in the street the prediction of a society of such technical perfection as to be truly frightening. He underscored how man, who was just about to wrest control of his exterior fate from Nature, was losing it to the machine. This scare, with its erstwhile literary coloring, has more recently grown in many quarters to a real horror in the face of the atom bomb and even more perfected instruments of destruction. The resulting deep-seated doubt about the benefits of technology must be remembered when we try to assess the climate in which present-day attempts to promote international welfare are being made. One indication of these doubts is the reiterated promise to preserve those additional values which peoples and cultures might possess; another is the increasing tendency to turn to the junior branches of science, the social ones, for insight into the human relationships and social processes which seem hitherto to have been omitted from calculations. Undoubtedly, these sciences are gaining momentum, but it is still a question whether they are fully equipped to help establish that international welfare so urgently wanted if our epoch is not to end in utter destruction.

NEW APPROACHES TO THE ESTABLISHMENT OF WELFARE PRIORITIES

The capital questions of goals and means for induced development measures, of expectations and effects, of complete or only partial success, are given increased attention in all circles concerned with initiating the new social change. They touch upon the whole interlocking system of the factors that determine the destiny of societies, their process of accelerated growth, their stagnation or downright disintegration. These interrelationships require profound study, and no effort should be spared to secure the best brains for the purpose.

It is high time we listened to the urgent call for organizing such studies on a wider scale. Yet the world cannot wait for the scientists. The underdeveloped countries do not want to wait a single day more. And as science is not unrelated to common sense, the planners of progress can move ahead fairly convinced that they are on the right track even if they can only take account in a general way of the experiences already gained. I shall devote this middle section of my paper to the two main guides to which practitioners have turned in recent years and which seem full of promise. They can be expressed by the terms "balanced development" and "community development." They are, really, *new* approaches to international social welfare, never before consciously attempted on a large scale.

BALANCED DEVELOPMENT

Despite the preponderance of economic *expertise* in technical assistance sought and given between countries, no responsible authority any longer holds that productivity is the only factor which needs to be changed and that welfare will automatically follow. On the contrary, it is more and more understood that, unlike the development of the Western world in the nineteenth century, the social as well as the economic mechanisms will have to be aided more systematically.

Already in 1949, when the Economic and Social Council voted the main resolution on an expanded Technical Assistance Program for economic development, with a budget outside the regular resources of the United Nations, the following clause was incorporated in the "Guiding Principles":

Requests for technical assistance may therefore be approved which will help governments to take account of the probable consequences of proposed projects for economic development in terms of the welfare of the population as a whole, including the promotion of full employment, and also to take account of those social conditions, customs and values in a given area which would directly influence the kinds of economic development that may be feasible and desirable. Similarly, requests may also be approved for technical assistance to governments desiring to undertake the specific social improvements that are necessary to permit effective economic development and to mitigate the social problems—particularly problems of dislocation of family and community life—that may arise as a concomitant of economic change.

In considerably stronger language this understanding of the need for more synchronized action in the social and economic fields is expressed in a general review of the first couple of years' experience of this program undertaken at the end of 1952, the so-called Wise Men's Report (i.e., the report of the four consultants appointed by the Executive Chairman of the United Nations Technical Assistance Board), which is regrettably not yet publicly available.

The same realization of the complexity of that development process with which planners have begun to tinker has so forcefully struck scientific circles that practically all the main social science disciplines—be it anthropology or economics, political science or sociology—have started to center conferences and speeches on this same topic of social change. This was already brought out at the international meeting of economists at Monaco, in September, 1950, a summary of which was published in the Spring, 1951, volume of the *International Social Science Bulletin*. Thus, for example, in one of the papers, "Some Aspects of Investment and Economic Development in the Continent of Africa," by S. H. Frankel, it immediately springs to the eye that the real problems in development cannot be isolated to the economic sphere. This is the same philosophy from which lately some special research institutes have grown, e.g., the Research Center in Economic Development and Cultural Change at the University of Chicago, and similar institutes at the universities of Pennsylvania and Cornell.

The emphasis upon the mutual interactions of economic and cultural or social development is beginning to run as an Ariadne thread throughout the literature on the subject, which in turn is growing at an encouraging speed,[3] and the stream of thinking is steadily becoming broader and deeper. But it is, as yet, as if we have been more successful in bringing to the surface an enormous number of problems than in finding solutions. This is in the nature of things. It is no criticism to point out that the best brains and the most experienced persons devoting themselves to the problem of promoting international social welfare are just finding out how immensely intricate the relations are.

One such new warning is against too facile a synonymizing of "poverty" and "underdevelopment"—or, in the antithesis, of "welfare" and "development." Even technically and economically advanced areas might still lack important aspects of welfare. And some of the so-called underdeveloped areas are not just underdeveloped, as is far too often imagined, in the sense of being in a virgin state waiting for the unfolding through new elements of technique, of resources that just lie fallow. This is an image derived from pioneer experiences, which, alas, is not an adequate pattern for most development work which lies ahead in the present world. We really want a new classification of countries as to the varying types in the development pattern. Many of the poorest countries are, as has been eloquently

[3] For a summary of this literature, see the two trend reports in *Current Sociology*, Vol. I, No. 4 and Vol. II, No. 4, published by UNESCO.

stressed by McKim Marriott, rather overdeveloped, i.e., exhausted. "In an over-developed area, too many techniques are too exhaustively applied by too many people to too little land." [4] He continues with a very timely warning that the problem of technological change in such an area is a question not only of adding something new but also of taking away something old. To strike a balance between what to give and what to take becomes a very delicate task indeed.

He illustrates concretely with his experience of India, the country which I prefer to use for exemplification in this paper, because from recent personal experience I can better visualize its development scene than that of many others:

The changes which had occurred had not penetrated very deeply but had gone far enough to double the population of the village in the past century. There is not now a spare square foot of land to be found. In the present generation, pastures and forest plots have all been cleared and sown with grain. While I was in the village, the last bits of interstitial land—roadways, cremation grounds, shade trees, gravel pits and the like—were leased out for cultivation. This was clearly desperation. Agricultural development has now gone so far that every new organic element is completely extracted from the soil once, twice, or many times each year. Almost every plant is fully used. Grass and weeds are carefully dug up, roots and all, to be used as animal fodder. Leaves are stripped off the trees repeatedly. The entire land lies absolutely bare and brown for three months of each year; the air, too, is brown, for it is full of the precious soil, dried and blown about as dust. I learned that one family of every ten had been compelled to leave the village in this generation in search of food.

If this warning was a general one against overoptimism in the transference of progress—Western style—it also touched upon

[4] McKim Marriott, "Technological Change in Overdeveloped Rural Areas," *Economic Development and Cultural Change*, December, 1952, p. 261.

another danger, the tremendous importance of which is just beginning to shake us, namely, the realization that the chief
factor threatening to unbalance development is that of population. The overpopulation scourge is the very symptom of an
unbalanced development. It is as if it were Nature's own revenge
when humans interfere in an unskillful way. The connection
is a simple one: some of the most easily instituted measures of
welfare lead to decreased mortality. This overthrows the balance
which at a very low existence level is upheld by high mortality
and high fertility checking each other. The result of the little
progress we have already seen instituted is being registered by
better and better instruments for census-taking all over the world
and it is being publicized as a great cause for pessimism, namely,
that the world population, and the population of the poorest
areas in particular, is growing fast. It is outgrowing the simultaneous, although slower, increase in food production. "The
hungry continents are getting hungrier."

The figures I quoted in my introductory section undeniably
point in this direction, and this is certainly of concern in our
attempts to increase welfare. For example, Ceylon has a population increase of nearly 2 percent annually. The direct cause can
be attributed to successful attempts at eradication of mass disease. It is, however, difficult to know if the high rate will persist.
If it does not, i.e., if the death rate again increases, such a
phenomenon testifies that *ad hoc* measures like spreading DDT
against malaria do not have long-term welfare effects if they
are not supported by sound improvements in environmental
sanitation, health services, etc., which would call for advances
also in other fields of welfare and the economy. If, on the other
hand, the beneficial effect on the death rate does persist, it would
testify that "welfare" has definitely been enhanced. But the
question would remain as to what factors were operative and,

in particular, whether economic production increased corre-spondingly? It would demonstrate that the whole equilibrium is threatened so long as fertility is not again made commensurate with the decrease of mortality.

It is in the realization of the tremendous implications of this race between population increase and food increase—to put the welfare problem in its simplest terms—that one country, India, has introduced a concerted effort at family planning in its Five Year Plan in order to ensure a balancing of development. I quote from the summary of the Plan which has been widely publicized within the country:

The rapid increase in population and the pressure on the limited resources available have brought to the forefront the urgency of problems of family planning. The main appeal for family planning is, however, based on considerations of health and welfare of the family. Family limitation or the spacing of the children is necessary and desirable in order to secure better health for the mother and better care and upbringing of the children. Measures directed to this end, therefore, form part of the public health programme.[5]

Quite considerable sums have been set aside for this activity. And a start is made which evidently meets with warm local response. A countryman of mine, the well-known demographer, Sten Wahlund, was recently called to India to evaluate the prospects and possibilities of a new program in this direction. His investigation, which covered an experimental area of 14 vil-lages and some 8,500 persons, resulted in a definite conclusion that the population was ready for the introduction of measures to limit its excessive growth. The majority of those who had three children wished no further addition to the family. This should be seen against the background of actual conditions: of

[5] *The First Five Year Plan: A Draft Outline* (Government of India Plan-ning Commission, July, 1951).

all women aged 14–40, 18 percent were pregnant; the average age of marrying was 13.8 years; at 25 years of age half the number of women were widows. And, to see it in social as well as in these individual terms: with a birth rate of 49.5 and a death rate of 13.5, the village must count on doubling its population in thirty years. But, the villagers said, ten years ago we could eat two meals a day, now we have only enough for one. And in the future?

I believe that these figures and examples, which have been culled from among the many available, tell more about measures needed for increasing welfare and for balancing the development than would anything I could add. This problem of the demographic threat, which may undo all our new efforts to raise the standards of living, has been here given primary attention because it reveals an effect certainly unparalleled and hitherto largely unsuspected. But there remains the more customary problem of how to initiate progress along such a wide front that balanced development surely follows—higher productivity, better health, and a raised educational and civic level of the population.

Insofar as systematic planning is attempted by the underdeveloped countries, there is nowadays a strong tendency toward comprehensive plans, as against "economic plans." This is a victory in terms of welfare. But very little is as yet known of how to introduce such broad changes in a strategic way. And the poverty of these countries—which is the most serious ill to be remedied—becomes the greatest obstacle. Let us again use India as an illustration, this time of the wider problem of how to initiate a balanced development. The Planning Commission of that country was so cognizant of this need, but also of the difficulty of choosing first things first in a systematic way, that a special chapter of the Draft Plan was devoted to "competing objectives."

Maximum production, full employment, lower prices, greater equality of income—all these—cannot, under certain conditions, go together. Each one of these objectives is, in itself, desirable, and there is, therefore, need for a balanced emphasis on each. A plan has, in other words, to work in terms of a scheme of priorities as between those objectives, laying more stress on some and less on others.

The conclusion is that in the pursuit of varied objectives, there emerges at each stage in a country's development, an optimum combination, and the task of economic statesmanship is to keep close to this optimum.

The practical conclusion for India was to give highest priority to an increase in the output of essential consumption goods, particularly food; further, to "fuller employment," by introducing more intensive agricultural methods:

Unemployed manpower has to be supported to-day by the rest of the community and it is, therefore, a factor depressing standards of living. Of all the corrosive factors in modern economic life, unemployment is probably the most serious.

Rapid extension of irrigation and the introduction of more intensive agriculture is the most important single step in the direction of remedying chronic under-employment.

Cottage and small-scale industries were not forgotten, as preference must be given, wherever technical conditions permit, to labor-intensive rather than to capital-intensive processes. Of the more long-run social objectives, the overriding one was a "reduction in economic inequalities" expressing the philosophy that

economic equality and social justice are conditions indispensable for the survival of democracy, and a carefully worked out policy for reduction of disparities in income and wealth is the *sine qua non* of planning.

As to the competition between possibilities referring to matters of more specific interest to social workers, it had to be laid down that the two most basic gains would have to be sought in education and health. This exclusion of more formal social services in the first stage was clearly accounted for by the limited resources:

Outside the activities relating to education and health there remains a large range and variety of socially necessary work which is bound up with the wellbeing of large sections of the community and will be an important element in its all-round progress.

The whole problem of competing objectives is worthy of very intense study. It is not only a question of a forced choice on account of scarce means but a question of understanding the development process, its intricate chain of mutually dependent processes, sometimes furthering, sometimes impeding each other. It is not a simple question of whether health should be given priority over education, not a question of one being more valuable than the other on any ladder of social values, but rather a question of whether a basis of education more easily leads to health than a basis of health leads to education—to express the matter in an oversimplified way. While any one country, like India, will attempt to strike its own balance, we should be ready to internationalize the problem and begin to assemble what we know about *strategy* in this whole interplay of social improvements.

How should it be done? There is here not so much to be learned directly from the countries already developed. First of all, we do not yet know whether they have a "balanced" development; we only know that the most violently unbalancing of all factors, the population factor, has been brought under tolerable control. Above all, we could not state that the process by which they became developed occurred in any balanced order. There are signs on the record book of stupendous costs paid in social maladjustment and human misery. But learning from that process and from all that could be unraveled by science's new practical field studies about interlocking relationships, we might hope to arrive at guidelines for the countries now entering the era of welfare. The ideal, of course, is to arrive at a veritable map showing what preconditions are responsive to which measure, the map also being supplemented by a kind of systematized and simplified timetable for development.

Although we are very far from having all the necessary scientific elements for making such a development map and accompanying timetable, may I nevertheless present a sketch of what the main stages in such a process would have to be, i.e., the type of measures to be introduced before others are taken and the type of measures to be introduced together.

Since all such attempts at identifying the phases of a development process must rely on certain assumptions and values, I have had to select some which I believe are most likely to correspond to those which will be adopted by most of the new countries if a conscious choice is made. The main *assumption* is that there will be only a minimum of outside capital available to the area under consideration and that gradual transition from one place to another thus becomes a necessary virtue; enough taxable income and saving for investment will have to be produced in the earlier stages to pay for advances toward the later ones. The main *value premise* which I have introduced, and one which is relatively rarely made explicit, is that a *sine qua non* for considering change as an improvement for society is that it increases and does not decrease human dignity or, more particularly, the opportunity for active participation of the population itself or, in one word, *democracy*. It might be argued that

material welfare could be increased more rapidly by other means
—perhaps by a combination of dictatorial exploitation of the
common means of production together with purposive breeding
and conditioning of a narrow elite to rule the enslaved masses
of productive workers. I have consciously chosen the very oppo-
site line with a minimum of coercion and a maximum of democratic control of the growth process, although it forces us to
wait for a sufficient education of the citizenry of a given area
before advancing to a level demanding more specialization.

The tentative chart below attempts to say that there are certain
types of measures which can be undertaken simultaneously and
certain others which will have to wait until a somewhat later
stage. If change were to be introduced in a very stagnant society,
with a growing population working scant land, there would be no
use looking immediately to industrialized Western society as a
model. Rather, a concerted attack would have to be made across
the categories in Stage I of the accompanying tabular analysis.
The primary reforms ought to be agricultural, concentrating on
populations living on farms, *without* moving them. They would
certainly be helped to increase the yield of their lands as well as
their handicrafts during off-seasons. They would be initiated into
a word of greater promise through education, "basic" or "fundamental," i.e., dealing with their own daily needs. They would
learn through this education some elementary rules of hygiene,
which they could apply henceforth to their own benefit; they
might even be inoculated against their specific variant of the
worst mass diseases. All this would require some visiting specialists, but not many innovations in the social structure. A stimulation to more cooperative undertakings in the economic field—
marketing, buying, and organized cooperation or building roads,
drilling wells—enters into the picture without disruption. The
way of organizing these improvements necessarily involves some

INSTIGATING REFORM IN STAGE I

Economic Measures	Education	Health	Social Welfare Policy	Professional Social Work	Political Organization	Administration
More food through agricultural improvements of seeds, of fertilizers, and of methods; local road building, irrigation devices; handicrafts	Fundamental education for adults with some by-effect of basic education for the children	Eradication of mass diseases; hygiene through environmental sanitation	Stimulation of cooperative enterprise and special community development projects (roads, wells, etc.)		Group meetings; extension of loyalties to interest groups rather than kinship or caste groups; village system of local responsible leadership encouraged	Streamlining central administration for channeling development measures

ADDITIONAL PROGRESS IN STAGE II

Economic Measures	Education	Health	Social Welfare Policy	Professional Social Work	Political Organization	Administration
Land reform; regional irrigation projects; local industries (cottage and scattered); commerce and transport extended to a wider region	Compulsory primary schooling	Child and maternity health services, including voluntary family planning	Schemes of planned saving; investment in housing and other local improvements; some taxation, some State loans	Social workers for development of social services centered on children and youth; also polyvalent assistance to local public bodies	Local self-government through specialized councils with community responsibility plus town meetings; extension of loyalty to larger community	*Centrally:* specialized administrative personnel (a) for planning and (b) for direction and control of specific fields mentioned. *Locally:* town clerk or specialized assistants to bodies of local self-government

ACHIEVING FULL DIVERSIFICATION IN STAGE III

Economic Measures	Education	Health	Social Welfare Policy	Professional Social Work	Political Organization	Administration
Adequate mechanization and rationalization of agriculture; trade, commerce, and banking; industrialization in specialized sectors	Technical and higher education; introduction of specialization within whole population with occupational and geographical mobility	Health controls; hospitals; psychiatric care and mental hygiene	Taxation on basis of income return; social insurance; trade unions and other national organizations of interest groups	Case work and specialized administration, serving local councils or other public bodies	Fully integrated local self-government; loyalties of national citizenship and international understanding	(Administration should intentionally be perfected in earliest stage)

group deliberations of the town meeting or local council variety. There would certainly be needed a considerable strengthening— in understanding, initiative, efficiency—of the central administration responsible for channeling this stimulation and any material aid that went along with it. The characteristic, however, of an auspicious primary stage in development is that people do not move but become stronger and more effective with their roots remaining in their local culture. For this purpose only little outside *expertise* is needed, the main role being played by those local or central authorities able to channel some of the most valuable innovations to their distant constituencies of human beings who have so far been underprivileged but whose scales of values have achieved their own equilibrium. This is not to say that development can occur without any sacrifice of tradition and values, but only that insofar as possible the transition should be gradual, allowing people to choose for themselves the newer ways of life.

The element of mobility which has to be introduced in order to further a more rapid economic development becomes the chief characteristic of a second stage. This should be taken quite literally: the generation succeeding the one to which the avenues of progress are first opened is the first which is at all prepared to move into new environments. They are now the young people who might be systematically schooled and who could thus be purposively prepared to extend their economic activities from the village to the market place, the transport system, the shops and factories of the region. This opportunity for wage-earning and cash income leads to a consideration of schemes for income utilization, for saving, for investment in housing and other amenities which make their lives more human. It also provides the opportunity for beginning taxation. And, let it be said, if saving and taxation schemes are not systematically outlined so as to fit this early phase of moneyed economy, all schemes subsequently introduced will appear as trickery and machination, without any firm anchor in popular understanding.

In this intermediary period of preparation for an even greater specialization and mobility, the structure of local government could reach its maturity. An increasing number of citizens would be available to serve in specialized functions, making up the school boards, the housing administrations, the cooperative combines which are necessary. With the growing complexity of society's affairs they would be ready to hire some administrative officers. I sincerely believe that they would be ready to see the value of having a capable town clerk on the one hand but also of availing themselves of the services of some social workers on the other hand to deal with the more personal aspects of their citizens' adjustment. Such social workers must be—for the interlocking reasons of scarcity and economy—of the polyvalent type which more and more of the underdeveloped countries are demanding. It is also my hope that social workers will be allowed to make one more specific and strategic approach to continued progress already at this stage: by concentrating on youth and children, they would help to lay the groundwork for a safe transition to the next phase of complex industrialization. They and their colleagues in the medical field who, for the same reason of finance, should concentrate on the young generation—since concentrate they must—would also serve to ensure a smooth developmental process by organizing advisory services for family problems. In many countries they would be requested to include advice on planned parenthood, so that families could have the number of children they definitely wanted and which they and society could hope to provide for.

It becomes superfluous to describe how the far-reaching specialization and high degree of social mobility which we connect with industrialization belongs to a third stage, presupposing the maturation process outlined in the other two. May it suffice to say that only with a differentiation of communities, urban and rural, and only with labor specialization and the utilization of national resources which can have competitive values on the economic market, can there exist the variegated society which calls for a really organized, first-rate system of social welfare as we know it. It follows that social workers, like all groups in the medical educational fields, will only in this stage get the full scope for their capacity to aid people and give the social system a richer content.

The value of a schematic presentation such as the one here attempted is that it should demonstrate how closely the measures interlock. It is intended to stress, for instance, that there is no possibility of introducing a nation-wide system of regular health control until a level has been reached where a rather important proportion of the population have incomes which leave a taxable surplus to pay for such services. The same is, of course, true with regard to any services which need to be instituted so as to reach each individual. There is no use introducing social security schemes until people have been conditioned, in a more primitive stage of moneyed economy, to distributing their earnings over longer time-periods, e.g., by a system of planned saving. There is no use—on the contrary, it involves very great risks of exploitation—introducing labor specialization on any far-reaching scale until considerable sectors have had an opportunity for vocational education, which presupposes that an even larger number have had an opportunity for primary schooling. Even land reform can only be an effective social change if a new form of local government and administration is ready to replace the old structure. Most of all, grave risks are incurred if active citizenship—through freely elected local councils and self-constituted cooperatives—

is not firmly developed at the level of the home community before great numbers of its population are drawn to urban centers where they would be exposed to becoming a proletariat of anonymous, uprooted street dwellers—the "pavement population" as they are often called in India. There the plight is so obvious that it hurts. This proletarianization is an unwanted result, of course, but it has happened so often in the history of industrialization, from Manchester to Johannesburg, that foresight must now be evoked to avoid it.

It goes without saying that no guide such as the one here sketched or the much better ones which will come out of the scientists' workshops could be applied wholesale or in any automatic fashion. First, the particular development stage of a given area within a country has to be ascertained at the outset. Only remnants of any country's map are still so untouched that they can start in Stage I; many measures will now have to aim purposively at Stage III, as the annals of Technical Assistance reveal. Most countries have wanted aid in order to push ahead such areas as were able to move from Stage II to Stage III. It will, however, often be found that even within one area developments have not kept the harmonious pace here outlined, but that in one domain they have leapt to a high level while lagging in others. The kind of unplanned urbanization now taking place in underdeveloped countries where cities are mushrooming in size is a case in point. If such unbalanced development has already occurred, curative measures are often needed alongside developmental ones, thus constituting a case for quite specialized social work, e.g., for work with juvenile delinquents, with rehabilitation of handicapped, with abandoned children and drunken vagabonds, at a much earlier stage of development than the "ideal" one tentatively set out above. The tabular analysis is admittedly too systematic but it is intended to be thought-provoking.

COMMUNITY DEVELOPMENT

India is deliberately chosen as the particular illustration showing present-day attempts to achieve a balanced development, in
order to lead directly to a second major consideration which I
want to stress at this juncture when the goal is international welfare. And that is that simultaneously with that wise foresight,
that planning of what from the national viewpoint is going to
ensure balanced development, the approach of building from
the bottom up should be utilized, starting with whatever individuals, families, villages, or communities can do to help themselves with the minimum of outside assistance and according to
their own preferences. This emphasis on the local aspect of
development, and on the motivation to active participation by
people themselves, was made the foundation of the system outlined above in the strong conviction that it is the only way to
ensure democracy in the new regions of the world.

Usually, when the community approach has been advocated as
the best road to development, it has been given a psychological
and cultural connotation and, as such, has perhaps too often been
held to be one that could be comfortably overlooked by economists and planners. As presented most coherently and profoundly
by Gandhi, it has even been judged as retarding rather than
promoting economic development. But if we go below productivity and ask for ultimate value premises, and if the reader
chooses as I do, namely, to increase the freedom and security
of the individual and to safeguard democracy by making it
a firm habit in the community, then this emphasis becomes
indispensable. In American phraseology, we see here the chance
of strengthening democracy at the grass roots, and that is where
it can most safely survive. We must never forget that this prob-

lem of the survival of democracy as such is far from solved in those regions of the world which are now being exposed to what we call modern civilization.

Mr. Nehru has stated the same concern in his deeply thoughtful and at the same time modest way in regard to the development plans for India. I quote from his inaugural addresses at the Development Commissioner's Conference on Community Projects, May 7, 1952:

Sometimes I begin to suspect and become a little afraid of these leads from the top that we, including me, are always giving. We have got into the habit of doling out good advice to everybody, to the country, to our people. Nevertheless, my own experience has shown that people who give too much advice are not liked. They irritate. . . . Obviously, it is necessary to plan, to direct, to organize and to coordinate, but it is even more necessary to create conditions where spontaneous growth from below is possible and can take place.

The awareness of this great challenge is growing. The schemes introduced to practice it are given many different names: in reality they are one and the same approach. Be it called "agricultural extension" or "fundamental education" or "health centers" or "social welfare centers," the basic idea is that of a community approach. As each of these betterment movements is also aware of the need for balanced development along several simultaneous lines, their interests quite naturally become widened so as to include measures from practically all fields, whether the start be made—and the label affixed—in medicine, agriculture, education, or social welfare. But it means that in some cases educators give medical advice or social centers give agricultural advice, and vice versa. This institutionalizing of community development schemes from separate vantage points is particularly symptomatic of *international* programs, while indigenous development schemes are often of a more generalized character. The United Nations provides assistance according to the specialization of its various organs; that is one reason for the variegated initiatives. But the machinery set up for coordination —and the burning desire of all concerned to serve the real needs of the people—are quickly overcoming this initial dispersion of effort. It can be safely stated that the United Nations is now actively working in this direction of integration of the specialists' interests, particularly by its evaluative surveys of all community development projects in certain areas and by cooperation between various organs which grows closer day by day.

Once more, the widest and most purposive activity in the direction of development starting with the communities is that flourishing in India since the end of the war and generally known under the name "community projects." Thanks to the vitality of the Gandhi movement, stressing village self-help and even village self-sufficiency, the ground was particularly well prepared in that country. The Five Year Plan is now concentrating all of those measures which are not intended for the industrialized sector on such village development schemes. A large-scale experiment in pioneering is also carried through under the direct supervision of the Planning Commission which—with some coopted members from ministries concerned—has established itself as a Community Projects Administration, responsible for concerted efforts in project areas embracing 16,500 villages. (This project is financed by the Indian government with support from the United States government and the Ford Foundation.)

The purpose of the Community Project shall be to serve as a pilot in the establishment, for the men, women and children, of the "right to live," food—the principal item in the wherewithal for this purpose, receiving the primary emphasis in the initial stages of the programme.

Evidently the project resembles most closely that of agricultural extension work, to talk in welfare terms familiar to the
United States. But it goes further:

A farmer in India has approximately six months of spare time in the
year. The landless labourer has approximately eight months in the
year running idle. If even a quarter of this idle time is used for building roads and schools, and in improving village drainage, creating
open parks and playfields and grazing grounds, digging compost pits
and attending to the thousand other necessities of life, the limited
Government finances provided for the project area can be multiplied
manifold.   **889904**

The objective of making a broadside attack on the common
problem of poverty, ignorance, and ill-health as interacting factors
is illustrated by the fact that the leading and administering person
is named "multi-purpose village level worker," as well as by the
fact that in each cooperating village there will be stationed for
some time a team—the so-called supervisory technical staff—of
specialists working side by side, e.g., one agriculturist, one public
health worker, and one educator.

It would be tempting to describe the daily approach to this
betterment work, which takes its start in wells and drainage, in
seeds and poultry, but also cares about education and domestic
hygiene and the strengthening of local leadership. It is truly a
"new" approach to welfare, in the sense that it is rather different
from the experience of the West, which has only started discussions on integrated welfare experiments when resources to
hand have been considerably more abundant. (The Peckham
center in England may be used to illustrate the localized counter-
part of the bold thinking that went into the Beveridge Plan as a
comprehensive national scheme—but one hundred years or more
after the development stage in which India, and several new
countries, are using it.)

Instead of a description, I will attempt to point up some of the more general problems of policy revealed by this approach, which is the one mighty new venture that seems to take root in the hitherto less developed countries.

One general point, which should be the object of much more scrutiny by economists and social scientists in general, is the extent to which this movement depends upon the supply of capital. The Indian scene is again valid for such a discussion of principle, there being in reality not one stream of thought—as may have been implied from my exemplification above—but two. One follows the Gandhian tradition, making a virtue of necessity and preaching the superiority of self-sufficiency. The raising of one's own sheep and the weaving of one's own garments, according to Gandhi's deep philosophy, works not only for the satisfaction of elementary needs but also for peace, since it leads to a state where nobody needs to haggle and bargain with anybody else, where nobody needs what the other one has; thus, where conflicts and tensions are minimized. It goes without saying that this approach to village development, which is implemented on a large scale in many considerable projects in India (quantitatively most important in the Firka Development Scheme in Madras State) is not only independent of outside capital but also of outside experts. The other line is illustrated by the Government Community Project and initiated by the now famous Etawah project, where the American town-planner, Albert Mayer, helped to introduce the "dirty hands method" on a large and purposive scale. In the Government project, there is some foreign capital and also some foreign experts, although less than outsiders usually believe.

Looking over the globe as a whole, one sees that there are considerably fewer occasions for aid by foreign workers in those community developments than the enthusiasm of social workers in more developed and fortunate countries might wish. But there is, of course, greater hope for a tenacious, long-term effort, the more the local resources are actively engaged in the efforts.

This leads me to suggest some specific distinctions between the various approaches, all utilizing composite teams, by professionals of various disciplines and various specialized agencies but directed rather by one group of specialists than another. "Agricultural extension" usually implies a start from the outside, by a technician not available in the local population, but working practically with them, very often only gradually extending from agriculture to other subject fields. "Health Centers" or "health demonstration areas" again denote a specialized initiative. Very often both of these approaches are related to central bodies of authority, which not only provide the necessary element of nonlocal administration but also plan and finance development and will continue to do so as a part of the perfected state machinery. "Fundamental Education," as the approach has been termed since the inception of the vast UNESCO program in this field, also is propelled by outside initiative except for two differences, a most decisive one being that it is conceived as a temporary measure—until primary schooling has become comprehensive—and another difference being that it is usually not endeavoring to perpetuate itself by any local or central administration. It is to be followed, to be sure, by institutionalized education, but is itself free from "officialdom." Besides, it has a goal per se outside the common goal of raising standards of living, namely, to aspire to a higher level of culture, a more lively spiritual existence, and is not to be seen as a means only to community development. I might dare to state also that the educational approach is the one most instrumental in bringing about self-help, as its very task is to increase the capacity for self-reliance.

"Community Centers" would seem to be the appropriate term, once the starting initiative is made by social workers. It is similar to Fundamental Education in the sense that from the outset it is linked to several specialized approaches, e.g., health needs merging with help needs. It is unlike the other types of initiative mentioned insofar as the techniques of social work employing "group work" and "community organization"—which are the terms utilized by social workers for the general stimulation of community improvement—are less of a specialization from the villagers' point of view, i.e., it offers less of a technique having the near-mystical prestige of knowledge unattainable by themselves. In point of fact, the villages often already possess a community organization which is vastly superior to any *ad hoc* initiation of leadership, namely, their local forms of self-government. And I have ventured to stress, particularly through my tabular analysis of progress, that it is this locally ingrained structure of leadership which carries the real chance of success even though it needs revitalizing by outside stimulation.

"Community Development Schemes," finally, is the generic term embracing all those varying efforts, and I am happy to report that the different professions are becoming more and more ready to forego their special approaches in favor of this integrated one of harmonious development.

I am not trying to judge, only to characterize, the various approaches and perhaps, indirectly, to issue a modest warning against overconfidence in organizing "uplift" movements from the outside. Stimulation, yes, and special techniques, yes. But we should conscientiously beware of any semblance of guardianship, the more so because very few groups will be found who do not have their own intricate and highly valued indigenous culture. Any idea of the widespread prevalence of primitive people unable to seek their own development must be abandoned. There exists no evidence whatsoever that intelligence is lacking. Poverty is to be aided, and aided strategically, but dignity is not to be impaired by any attempt to manage these people or determine their destiny for them.

On the other hand, I dare to hold out a promise of considerable success for those projects having strong indigenous roots. And here again enters the cardinal point: that of local responsibility, the idea of local self-government, of free and direct democracy. In several of the countries now most active in stepping up their development pace and most conscious of the process that it involves, the two main instruments used at the local level are the cooperatives for the economic activities and the village council for the general run of municipal affairs, including political, administrative, and often judicial and educational functions. The existence of the age-old Panchayats in India and the persistent attempts to revitalize them, as well as parallel efforts to rescue similar residuals of primordial democracy in other countries, is one of the most encouraging signs. When some self-activating body responsible for the local planning of development exists (and I do not mean sporadic or spontaneous leadership, and still less extraneously inspired leadership, but the exercise of a public responsibility by somebody elected by his cooperative or his constituency), then the foundation for further welfare progress is most safely laid. Then also the outside experts might come and go and be what they should be: experts with certain techniques which so far are rare in the environment. They would be liberated from the unbearable responsibility of acting for the people, of choosing their lines of future destiny.

The newest approaches for international stimulation to improve welfare are of this kind: the local populations become more and more eager to take their fate into their own hands, to organize for their common benefit improvements in the levels of living, security, and happiness. But they still need a lot of knowledge about the strategy of achieving their ends. And they look to the more fortunate countries and to the international community to get it.

TOWARD AN INTERNATIONAL SCIENCE OF SOCIAL WELFARE

The problems described by illustrations in the preceding section and listed as definite queries in the introductory section have only to be raised in order to cause anxious concern about the "exportability" of the technical know-how in the social field. In the early days of enthusiasm for Technical Assistance, it was taken for granted both that the knowledge existed and that it was exportable. The very fact that some countries were "developed" seemed to bear witness. But those of us who have been placed in some position of responsibility for providing information about the general knowledge on which special measures for inducing development may be based (for "briefing," to speak officialese), quite early shuddered, as we knew that against the giant needs, the craving on the part of the underdeveloped countries for sharing the world's capital of know-how, there could be offered only some odd elements of knowledge kept together by guesswork.[6]

THE EXPORT AND IMPORT OF KNOW-HOW

The aid from more to less developed countries has been visualized as an export of technical knowledge, a sharing and an equalization of the world's capital of knowledge. It may be

[6] A searching self-analysis of Technical Assistance experts who have first-hand experience of the difficulties in the field and who have discussed them with a group of social scientists will be found in *Social Aspects of Technical Assistance in Operation,* published by UNESCO in 1954.

well worth scrutinizing this whole notion in regard to social welfare from a scientific point of view. In order not to make too general and too sweeping statements of exportability and importability as such, I would like to use the case of the United States as an illustrative example.

What could the world first and foremost expect from the United States, the country that undeniably has realized the highest level of productivity? Which of its techniques are particularly in demand?

The question is much more difficult than appears at first. Just because the development level in most countries at the receiving end is so grossly different, they cannot benefit from many of the specific techniques of this country. This is particularly true with regard to social welfare patterns—leaving to the market of exportable and highly desirable knowledge the whole realm of engineering and specific techniques in medicine, agriculture, and every branch of practical knowledge. But social welfare has in the United States, at least at the outset, been of the type of individualized approach rather than of broad mass measures in terms of social policy. The undisputed superiority of this country in the social work field lies exactly in that kind of technique (case work, individual placing of foster children, readaptation of the handicapped, juvenile courts, marriage counseling, etc.).[7] But that

---

[7] Individual placing of foster children only takes on importance when children really start to be intentionally placed. In most poor countries the village solidarity is enough to keep them. But if, as does happen even in poor countries, an attempt is made to build institutions, the new American advances in knowledge about foster children becomes important, partly as an argument against institutions and for family placement, partly for improvement of the institutional environment. Similarly with regard to juvenile courts. In most countries a knowledge of the ecological conditions for youth behavior and, if possible, a systematic improvement of the environment as such is indicated far more than the instituting of courts. But if brutal penal methods have been introduced, the corrective influence of American knowledge about corrective measures with regard to juvenile delinquency should be welcome.

is precisely the kind of technique from which the most under-developed countries can as yet least benefit. They cannot muster the resources, either in terms of finance or of personnel, for implementing it. And they are often not individualized in their own psychology. An interesting example is the experience made by persons with an acuteness of anthropological observation: that in many places a Western type of doctor fails because he does not understand that the patient might have to be accompanied by his whole family or by some group from the village, according to hierarchical behavior patterns, instead of coming alone to a consultation. The psychological individualization for which American social work tradition is justly famous will only come into its own when a certain level of development has been reached.

I would, however, certainly not want to be made responsible for reducing any interest in the individualized social welfare techniques if the interest has spontaneously sprung up. And I would most strongly urge their immediate introduction, say, in a metropolis where maladjustment has already resulted from the incipient change. But I must conclude from the wide experience registered by social science that this is not particularly the type of social welfare measure adequate to meet the mass needs of most underdeveloped countries just now. One look at their national plans and their own village efforts shows us another way. The reminder given in the previous section of the gradual construction of a coherent social policy and the need to rely for its furtherance on the taxation of the people themselves also forces us to look at other types of welfare patterns as fundamental, symbolized in cooperatives and self-help projects on one hand, mass measures against disease and for education on the other hand. These are, however, to culminate as quickly as possible in certain measures for a better guarantee of incomes on the part of the national community, which calls for social security, and in remedial, readjusting measures for all individuals or families trapped by particular misfortune, which makes the case for social work proper. However, the peculiar history of this great country of the United States—first developing great wealth and then applying itself to social problems—makes it less imitable than the history of some other countries which have had to build their social measures slowly and steadily on a basis of indigenous, more egalitarian poverty, which has thus been overcome by more synchronized action in the economic and social spheres.

Although the exportability of the specifically American types of social welfare measures is questioned for the earliest stages of development, it may be powerfully asserted that the getting-rich technique of this country is so much the more appropriately exportable. And there is certainly a great truth in it. In all that is related to increased productivity, to labor-saving and labor-specialization, to engineering and construction, there is more to learn from this country than from any other. It is, therefore, quite logical that you should find spread over the globe a considerably greater number of American engineers than American social workers. But increase in economic well-being depends not only on the machine but also on the man. And when it comes to incentives that govern man's efforts at productivity, or when it comes to the organization of business, it is safest to realize that the underdeveloped world is not very like the American scene, or any Western country for that matter. It is not even to be taken for granted that the world wants to become Western in this sense. We must never forget that there might be deep differences in values between the countries that developed early and those that developed late; it is not even to be assumed that it would be to the good of the world if incentives became the same everywhere, that is, if only one set of values survived.

There is, however, another sector where American superiority is indisputable, where one might almost speak of a surplus that could be shared with others to the great benefit of the world. So I can appropriately conclude this excursus, which has frankly been somewhat an *argumentum ad hominem*, by pointing to the desirability that the propensity for cold and skillful observation of social facts, for incisive analyses of social relationships, which are abundantly available in this country, be given world-wide application. *Its advance in social science might be America's greatest gift to the art of international social welfare.*

THE NEEDS FOR SOCIAL SCIENCE AND SOCIAL TECHNOLOGY

This examination of problems of exportability as related to one country with a rich fund of development knowledge, the preceding description of development needs and development experiments in underdeveloped countries, and the introductory listing of certain dangers imminent in our present attempts to give technical assistance from the West for induced social change elsewhere have all led to a series of claims for *more knowledge*. These claims may be summarized in the following list of queries:

1. How much exists in the form of a systematic analysis of preconditions and potentialities in various countries and cultures, which could be used for prognoses of their inherent development forces and for judging what the impact of new elements might be?

2. How much exists in the form of a generalized, theoretical knowledge about economic, social, and cultural change, and particularly about their interdependence (in order to prescribe such timing of measures that a balanced development can be assured)?

3. How much exists of a thoroughgoing international com-

parison and evaluation of measures, actually put into practice, for improvement of social welfare?

4. How much exists of a scientific approach for evaluating change resulting from the importation of such measures?

And to turn from basic research to technology:

5. How much exists in the form of simplified practical knowledge, founded on the scientific explanations listed above, which would make possible a veritable technique of social planning?

Not too much should be expected because social science itself is only in an early stage of development. But let us go through the list of possibilities:

1. To establish a firm base line of *status quo ante*, against which to measure subsequent change, must be the primary concern. That means that we must possess scientifically valid knowledge about existing social conditions, cultural patterns, and ongoing processes of growth in the varying regions of the world. This basic science about the cultural context has made rapid progress in recent years and is one of the truly encouraging features of social science. Whether it be called cultural anthropology, as in this country, or social anthropology, as in Europe and particularly in Great Britain, it is beginning to fill the white spots on the world's map with understanding descriptions of the divergent ways of life, the local means for satisfying vital needs, the value systems and thought ways of the manifold variations of the human race. Increasingly, the science of anthropology is also being utilized to provide firm basic information for practical endeavors to bring change to regions where change is desired. I need not here enumerate all such attempts of policy-makers to have recourse to anthropology; I might just refer to the interest given to this science at the time of the occupation of Japan. The colonial authorities in France and Belgium, as well as Great Britain, are increasingly utilizing the services of anthropologists

and, with them, related scientists for surveying local conditions, in attempts to arrive at a more objective appraisal of situations in Africa, the West Indies, and other parts of the world. Also the Technical Assistance authorities are beginning to give some attention to this need for a base line survey of preconditions. In the UNESCO Technical Assistance mission to Liberia, an anthropologist was included at the explicit request of the Liberian government.

This leads me to ask whether what is done is enough or whether we should not state specific demands for improvements. To this it must be summarily said that what is done so far remains a beginning only. Not merely quantitatively, because there are still *terrae incognitae*, but because existing knowledge is, despite heroic efforts on the part of individual scholars, *spotty*. There is a survey team visiting a village here, a tribe there, a community or a region. But the systematic and coherent over-all view is not yet achieved; comparisons are still difficult to establish and therefore systematization of the knowledge has not yet developed to the point where we can say that the base line is firmly established.

Next, what is done tends to be more static and descriptive than dynamic, for the simple reason that comparisons over periods of time have rarely been made as yet. We all take delight in the recent projects for "villages revisited"—like Lewis's re-appraisal of the Mexican village Tepoztlan twenty years after Redfield's study of it.[8] But this is still a far cry from observational sequences on the changes that are constantly going on. Still on the waiting list for the young geniuses who must be flocking to this science of the future is the establishment of trends of growth, of time series for the change in the various factors involved in

[8] Oscar Lewis, *Life in a Mexican Village, Tepoztlan Restudied* (University of Illinois Press, Urbana, 1951).

welfare, in patterns of cooperation, in beliefs. Such a dynamic approach is all-important, if science is to be applied to action.

May I add, as a recurrent intrusive theme that, of course, this rapidly developing science of the cultural context is as yet characteristically *foreign*. It is somewhat in the nature of things: we humans are curious about the unknown rather than about what is familiar. So "we" study Africa, while the Africans have hardly felt the spur to study themselves (or to study us!). I am not going to "sermonize" that each country ought to study itself —although I do believe that there is a great value in taking a scientific attitude to one's own problems and that there is a definite need to promote social science within each country. But also, there is, in this task of mapping the pre-existing social conditions everywhere and establishing the great fan-pattern of curves of already ongoing change, an imperative need to pool internationally all that is being learned, and to arrive at a stage where there is full cooperation for the sake of interpretation by those studying and those being studied, i.e., by foreign and domestic social scientists together.

2. There is, however, also need for a more specific science, or rather a coherent *theory of social change*, if we are to be able seriously to attack the problem of international social welfare. What measures lead to which effects? What changes in nutrition lead to which changes in the economic sector, and vice versa? What quantity of extended education is befitting to the particular constellation of social circumstances existing in a given country —questioning whether too little education may be an obstacle to raising productivity and whether too much may lead to unsatisfied aspirations and social unrest? This is just a "pick" at some of the highly important practical problems which are capable of getting theoretical guidance for their solution, but which have so far hardly more guidance than there is in posing

the questions, thus alerting the attention of those concerned.

During the last few years, a number of field studies have been begun with a view to following the process of change itself and trying to establish the interrelationships between the various factors which have to interplay if we want to promote welfare.[9] But so far very little has been done by way of systematic comparison between the spot studies or by way of weighing up the evidence in order to arrive at *conclusions* at varying levels of universal validity. This is understandable, as the process of theorizing could not be the job of one man or even one team. When mentioning previously the recognition of the need for balanced development, I referred to some wider, collective attempts which have been made to arrive at a synthetization. First, the economists touched upon it at their international meeting in 1950; the International Economic Association continued by placing the questions of the Meaning and Criteria of Economic Progress on the agenda for their round-table discussion in Italy in the summer of 1953. Our own UNESCO *International Social Science Bulletin* has recently devoted a special issue to Social Implications of Technological Change,[10] but it only begins to broach the subject. In order to provide the first tools for international comparisons we are also beginning to publish some international bibliographies, the first one with a trend report of studies on technical inventions as spark plugs for social

[9] I need here only refer to two important centers in the United States: Cornell University's program for research and training in culture and applied science (see *Human Problems in Technological Change*, a casebook edited by E. H. Spicer [Russell Sage Foundation, New York, 1952]) and Chicago University's Research Center in Economic Development and Cultural Change, which publishes the periodical *Economic Development and Cultural Change*.

[10] *International Social Science Bulletin*, Vol. IV, No. 2, 1952 (English and French editions, New York, Columbia University Press).

change, appearing in our bibliographical periodical *Current Sociology*.[11]

Realizing how utterly inadequate are these few first attempts, we are gratified to see some progress being made toward the establishment of a true international research center for this very field. The Economic and Social Council of the United Nations has since 1946 been concerned with a project for establishing international research laboratories for problems of such a nature that they cannot be efficiently dealt with by national or private research. The UNESCO General Conference has now twice voted that such a research center should be created for studying the "Social Implications of Technological Change," as it was phrased. Although it has not voted the corresponding funds necessary, a beginning is being made; plans are being laid and interested cooperation is mobilized on the part of scientists all over the world to participate in the work of an International Research Office under UNESCO auspices in Paris, provisionally carrying out some of the work of the planned international research center. And no problem is in greater need of an international approach than that of the interrelationships of economic, cultural, and human factors in social change. It is a problem where the factual evidence is being produced by the efforts of individuals and large combines of scholars in some countries, but where the theoretical structure is as yet lacking. The situation is about the same as if the science of physics were all observations and no laws. This may sound categorical, and I do not intend to underestimate such pioneer studies as are now under way. But in comparison with the giant experiment which we are dedicated to undertake, that of internationalizing social well-

[11] *Current Sociology*, Vol. I, No. 4, 1952 (Bilingual edition, New York, Columbia University Press).

being, it must be said to be fatal that we have so little of this systematic knowledge of what effects to expect.

3. Turning now more directly to the question of the measures we want to utilize, of social welfare techniques we want to introduce, the situation is somewhat similar to the one just described. There exists an abundance of reports on social welfare systems in various countries, as well as collections of legislative details and manuals for handling special social work techniques. But what are they related to—judged from the international angle? What preconditions in society do they suppose? What economic development stage are they fitted to? What is their margin for flexibility in varying cultural situations? The whole question of their transference is practically without study.

It should be noted that even in that most scrupulously careful preparatory work which the International Labor Organization is devoting to the presentation of any of its recommendations, there is no presentation of a scientific—experimental or observational —*comparison* of the systems employed in different countries: their preconditions, their reception by public opinion, and their effects.

Could there be such a science? There could certainly be a beginning of one. But probably only under the aegis of the United Nations or its Specialized Agencies. Because who else would be interested in being an arbiter in the struggle for prestige which undeniably is involved when one country or another believes in the exportability of its own welfare prescriptions?

It was an early ambition of mine, publicly expressed at the time when I was serving the Social Affairs Department of the United Nations, that the United Nations should build up such a powerful storehouse of knowledge of social welfare techniques from the whole world. In all fairness it should be said that insofar as the descriptive side of such work is concerned, the United

Nations is doing a great deal, as is the International Labor Organization in its specialized field. For countries, or individual experts who want to borrow ideas or check on the precedents for their own use, these collections of provisions in force are undeniably of considerable value. They are also a basis for all further international pooling of experience. But now is the time to proceed to the truly scientific task. As a minimum the internationally available store of knowledge should include—since field experiments must be excluded—a systematic listing of all welfare measures and a specific comparison of the preconditions; the popular reaction to, and understanding of, measures when introduced; an analysis of their interdependence or relation to measures of an economic and legal character (e.g., marriage loans in relation to marriage counseling, to prevailing rates of interest, and to legislation about marriageable age); and, finally, of their effects under varying cultural conditions.

In other terms, it should be expected that the United Nations or some other central international agency should provide such massive evidence of failure or success of various methods that each time a nation planned a reform, it should, when choosing among alternatives, have available a summary of the experiences of other countries. And that summary should be so easily available in printed texts that every country could borrow and copy it as an "international introduction" to all national texts on specific reforms.

Of course, we are far from having such ready-made summaries and we are as yet very far from having the scientific evidence available. I would go further and stress as an astonishing fact that there does not exist an *international science of social policy*.

Neither does there exist any nongovernmental organization that purposively works on it. It gives food for thought that while international comparisons of law have given rise to a special

International Committee of Comparative Law and while, of course, economics has a tremendous superstructure of international research, nothing parallel exists in the field of social welfare policy.[12] It might well be asked if this would not be a proper objective for the International Conference of Social Work, which would then have to be given considerably larger resources. If that organization is too close to professional interests—being a body of social workers and practitioners rather than policy-makers and scientists—one would have to look in the sky for an International Academy of Comparative Social Policy.

4. I have so far been dealing with the three branches of scientific research basic to a purposeful development of social welfare on a universal scale—a complete cultural anthropology, a theoretical science of social change, and a comparative one of social welfare policy. But science does not prescribe what to do; its function is only to reveal which conditions actually exist and what is likely to be the effect of introducing new elements in the existing social fabric. And science is, after all, fairly inaccessible to the practitioner as well as to the policy-maker. What is needed between social science and social action is a technology. Let me for the sake of brevity call it the technology of planning, taking planning in its broadest sense as intentional introduction of change for the purpose of certain goals. These goals have so far been left out of this context. It has become a popular refrain, known to all of us, that science does not postulate the values. It will be for the national authorities or for the interested citizens' groups to state them, to give specific body and soul to the term welfare, hitherto used far too loosely. Then it would be for the technology of planning to make the connection between those

---

[12] It should not be overlooked that some teaching institutes, like the New York School of Social Work, are pioneering in comparative studies of this kind. But there still needs to be international recognition of this as an important new branch of science.

specific goals and what science may have to say about various ways and means to achieve them, about various side-effects of these measures and also their applicability in the specific cultural constellation of the environment, about considerations of timing and of sequences between one measure and another.

5. I am quite convinced that if we only had the basic sciences developed as depicted, there would soon follow a technology of immediate usefulness to policy-makers and practitioners. Elements in such a social technology should be the elaboration of *techniques for evaluation,* for actually measuring the success of measures as applied. In this as in all the other fields a beginning is being made. It is fascinating to follow the many attempts undertaken in our time to assess the results of our own social experimentation. In national endeavors such assessment has become quite common, particularly in this country through using follow-up interviews, and in some other countries through statistical indices showing in considerable detail improvements—for instance, in the quotient of overcrowding in housing. On the *international* level something similar is only about to begin. Particularly praiseworthy seems to me the attempt undertaken by the United Nations to give us a general international survey of existing social conditions and to assess the efficiency of community development schemes. The education to objectivity also in social affairs, the readiness to self-criticism, and the concern for efficiency which are involved in all these endeavors are a very wholesome influence in the social welfare field. It is not belittling the values won if I have to point out that so long as the basic scientific investigations are not made, these attempts refer to practical appraisal rather than to specific evaluation, which should measure the direct effects and by-products in a very intricate pattern of causation, as yet not revealed to us. A most interesting experiment to establish the scientific bases at the same time

as the evaluation techniques proper is just now under way in India, by special courtesy of the Ford Foundation, which organizes evaluation teams of young Indian social scientists to follow from the first minute certain pilot projects of village development. And UNESCO is carrying out an assignment to assemble the knowledge already available in the field, hoping to provide useful guides and scientifically tested evaluation techniques for several types of social action programs (fundamental education, schemes for exchange of persons, etc.).

Wider still, however, are the claims for a technology of planning. The estimate of efficiency should, preferably, be available before, and not only after, an experiment in development. And may I again underline the urgency of establishing such an international body of knowledge by a reminder that the planners do not wait. There is all over the world a full-speed activity under way to plan for increased productivity, improved health, raised standards of well-being. There is a definite craving that such planning should be the responsibility of the peoples themselves, yes, that it should to a certain measure be planning for independence, against too great a dependence. So much the more urgent is it therefore that the technical resources for executing this planning be available and that a "social technological institute," if I may express it so, be available for training planning experts from all lands. Not to let them acquire that knowledge is going to be very unwise. Because however eagerly a country welcomes capital from another country and however generously it copies models, techniques, and know-how for developing various sectors, it will not want anybody to do its own thinking. In the incipient stage in which we now find ourselves, the risks are that those who come with gifts—whether in the shape of material aid or technical know-how—also influence a number of decisions on the destiny of the new countries. There is also another risk that the national policy-makers have very general plans of their own, that they have clearly formulated goals as to the welfare they want and the path their peoples will have to travel, but that they have not the next rank of experts who should have to judge, synchronize, and institute the measures needed, nor those who can interpret to the people the complex path of gains and sacrifices which follow any change.

I sincerely hope that I shall not be charged with overstating the case for science by making things more complicated than they are. The contrary is the case: the whole of our present-day attempt to improve the welfare of all people is so much more complicated—not difficult, but intricate—than we thought when we dedicated ourselves, through our countries and through the United Nations, to the task. The changes which are to be introduced do not present themselves as self-evident, or as simple, or as cheap.

In terms of money alone, the sharpened foresight which science can give may well be worth-while. The failure of one or two multi-million-dollar projects, or even smaller ones, is enough to demonstrate that knowledge is so far incomplete.

But considerations much more delicate and costly than money matters are involved. Practically all changes for social betterment touch the realm of human values, families, traditions, religions. We certainly must have all the reassurance possible that we are not disrupting matters of greater value to those concerned than the new material gains we might help to introduce. And, even if we need not think too pessimistically in terms of actual change—large parts of the world being so truly at the bottom of subsistence that change is rather destined to be in the direction of uplift—we must still remember that the efforts spent should be without undue waste of money, time, or of the confident expectancies of the many who have hoped against hope for such a long time. Only if we pool from all countries what we already know and all that we with some minor sacrifice of money and organization could get to know, may we rest assured that wisdom matches the good will which already exists to promote the ever increasing welfare of all peoples.

TRAINING FOR
INTERNATIONAL
RESPONSIBILITIES

At the very outset of any exploration of training in connection with international social welfare activities one is immediately confronted with this fundamental question: how is it possible for American social work to make any real contribution to promoting social welfare in the so-called underdeveloped countries, since American social work has developed in response to the social needs of a highly developed, highly organized, and highly prosperous nation?

Doubting Thomases will say and do say that the people in these underdeveloped countries are in need not of refined social services but of the bare necessities of life. If this criticism is valid then it is useless for us to spend any time discussing training in the field of international social welfare. Certainly we must recognize that fully half of the 2,400,000,000 human beings in this world go to bed hungry; that half of these human beings are suffering from preventable disease; that countless millions have no shelter; and that two thirds are unable to read or write. From a world-wide standpoint we in the United States and in a few other countries are only islands of plenty in a sea of human misery.

It is true that misery has been the lot of far too large a portion of mankind for far too long a time. There is nothing new about this. But what is new is that we of the democracies have preached the gospel of the innate dignity and worth of every human being and this gospel has spread to the farthermost corners of the world. Moreover, we of the free world have demonstrated conclusively that human misery is not inevitable, that it is possible for mankind to improve its material lot far beyond the wildest dreams of our forefathers. Is it then any wonder that poor people everywhere believe that their lot should be and can be improved?

The result has been that in underdeveloped countries throughout the world, governments have come into power pledged to carry out sweeping economic and social programs. No one who has had an opportunity to observe the courage and zeal with which many of these governments are undertaking their herculean tasks can help but be deeply impressed.

I believe that American social work has a great contribution to make in facilitating the social organization necessary for this economic development and for maximizing the social good made possible by such economic development. I believe further that American social work has a great contribution to make in convincing the common people of a country that a united effort is being made to improve their lot and that they are significant participants in that effort. And let us not forget the supreme importance of enlisting and sustaining the understanding and support of the common people, because the road to a better life is a long and a hard one at best. Justice Holmes once said: "I find the great thing is not so much where we stand as in what direction we are moving. To reach the port of heaven we must sail sometimes with the wind and sometimes against it; but we must sail and not drift, nor lie at anchor." [1] The common people must be convinced that they are sailing, even if it be slowly, in the right direction and that it is their ship. Otherwise the inevitable lapse of time between the promise of democracy and the achievements of democracy is likely to result in chaos and disaster.

When I say that American social work has a great contribution to make in this field of international welfare, I am thinking of the basic principles underlying American social work and the various ways those basic principles have already been applied or can be applied. I recognize, as do all of us, that the actual practice of social work is dependent upon the economic, social, political, and cultural milieu in which it is practiced. I am sure all of us also recognize that much of the specialization that has developed in the practice of social work in this country is not feasible in undeveloped countries. But, while some of the practice of social work in this country may not be exportable, all of the principles and the basic methods, if they are sound, are universal in their application, because human beings everywhere have common human needs, common human motivations, and belong to the common brotherhood of man. As I see it, our task as social workers is to assist responsible individuals, particularly in these underdeveloped countries, to apply sound social work principles to the immediate economic and social problems with which they are confronted.

Before I discuss some of the considerations that I think should be kept in mind to assure that we are meeting our international responsibilities as effectively as possible, I should like to indicate

[1] Quoted in letter from Josephus Daniels to President Franklin D. Roosevelt, dated January 1, 1936. In Carroll Kilpatrick (ed.), *Roosevelt and Daniels* (Chapel Hill, University of North Carolina Press, 1952), pp. 159–60.

broadly what international responsibilities American social workers are being called upon to assume. One of the most far-reaching is the training in the United States of the many social workers from other countries. Literally thousands of American social workers—teachers, administrators, practitioners—are participating in this great mutual exchange of ideas as these international observers and trainees visit our social welfare agencies and study in our schools of social work throughout the country. A very large percentage are short-time visitors who come for a few weeks to observe a variety of programs related to their special interest. However, I am particularly concerned with the increasing number who come for specific training covering a period of several months to a year. Many of them come under the United Nations fellowship and scholarship programs, or under one of the United States technical assistance programs, or through the voluntary agencies. They come in increasing numbers from the less-developed areas of the Far East, the Middle East, Africa, and South America.

Judging by the group of trainees for whom the Social Security Administration has planned, the general educational preparation of the group as a whole is excellent, only a handful not having an undergraduate degree. Many have a graduate degree, a considerable number having a doctorate. A very large percentage of these people hold executive or supervisory posts in their national welfare ministries or in major local welfare agencies. About one sixth are directors of schools of social work or members of school faculties. Some of these come for training in a social work specialty such as child welfare, medical social work, psychiatric social work, or social work educational methods. The majority, however, come for general social work training. An increasing proportion are concerned with community organization and social administration.

In addition to these training responsibilities here at home, social workers are now serving as welfare advisers throughout the world. Overseas missions of the United Nations and the United States Point Four program, as well as the important voluntary national and international services, are including social workers, sometimes as part of a team concerned with broad economic development programs. In these programs the social worker has, as his partner in planning, the doctor, the engineer, the educator, and the agriculturalist.

I will mention only one or two other major areas in which we find American social workers active. The social welfare programs of the United Nations, the International Labor Organization, and international voluntary organizations have, in addition to their field services and fellowship opportunities, important functions of research and standard-setting. The subject matter ranges from broad studies of standards of living to development of specific social services and social legislation. American social workers have had an opportunity to contribute to international social welfare philosophy, standards, and methodology through international meetings of expert groups, such as working parties, seminars, and the like, where representatives with different backgrounds and experience in social welfare come together to exchange ideas and recommend new programs and standards. Through the United Nations Social Commission, social workers have contributed in a wide variety of fields. The United States delegation has given constant and strong support to studies of, and the development of standards in, the fields of social welfare administration, community organization, and training for social work.

Likewise at large international meetings, such as the International Conference of Social Work, American representation has been substantial and its contribution characterized by interest in relating social welfare developments to improving standards of living throughout the world.

In all this international exchange of knowledge and in the development of studies, the American contribution has been made possible through the cooperation of social welfare experts in both the governmental and voluntary agencies. The Federal agencies working closely with state welfare agencies and with the voluntary agencies, through arrangements made by the National Social Welfare Assembly, have been able to put forward for international consideration the experience of a wide variety of social developments in the United States.

TRAINING THE FOREIGN STUDENT

When we turn our mind to this question of training social workers so that they may function effectively in the field of international social welfare activities, we are confronted with certain special problems.[2] It is necessary that we cope with these special problems and solve them without distorting the normal functioning of either the school or the cooperative agencies.

We must recognize above all that the people who come here for training need to be helped to understand our particular social, economic, political, and cultural institutions. They need to know what our social needs are and how we attempt to meet these needs. This calls for special advisory services, for special orientation arrangements, and for more extensive and intensive observational opportunities than in the case of American students.

[2] For the characteristics of students and the nature of social work training available in other countries, see: *Training for Social Work* (Department of Social Affairs of the United Nations, 1950); *Social Workers from around the World Observe Social Welfare in the United States* (Social Security Administration, Washington, D.C., 1952); *International Students in Schools of Social Work in the United States* (Social Security Administration, Washington, D.C., 1953).

We should also bear in mind from the very outset that our educational methods themselves are quite different from those to which these students from abroad have been accustomed. Most of them are accustomed to the straight lecture method. When they are confronted with the discussion method they may well be bewildered and uncertain, not only as regards themselves, but as regards the principles and processes so freely examined. Therefore, it is necessary that we be particularly careful to help these students organize their ideas and conclusions as they proceed with their studies. At the same time we must be sure not to encourage any tendency to seek the "right" answers without thinking through problems for themselves.

In order that these students can carry out effectively their heavy responsibilities when they return home, they will need to know what is involved in program development, not simply how to work effectively with individual clients. But by the same token they must not be permitted to overlook the importance of case work, not only for illuminating basic concepts and methods, but also for the basic skills needed for working with people which are involved in all social work.

All of this requires sympathetic understanding, careful planning, and painstaking explanation in assisting these students with their school work and field work. Some of them in their desire to be of maximum usefulness when they return home will want to "cover the water front," taking altogether too many courses and too heterogeneous a schedule of field work. Others, motivated by the same desire, will want to concentrate unduly on some one aspect of social work which seems to them of particular and immediate value to their local community or national government. There is greater chance of success in helping them to acquire basic social work training if this motivation is appreciated and channeled effectively.

The problem of assisting these students to undertake a well-balanced and interrelated program is not confined entirely to students coming from countries with relatively underdeveloped social welfare programs. Students coming from countries with well-established programs many times are unduly interested in learning about the organization and procedures involved in our social legislation and in our community welfare programs rather than in basic social work training. Therefore, they too need wise and understanding counsel.

We must admit that our task in assisting these students from abroad with their programs is considerably lightened if the curriculum itself is well balanced and interrelated and truly generic. Otherwise it will be difficult to persuade students who will be leaders in the community development programs and administrators of national social legislation when they get back home that they should study anything except group work, community organization, or social administration.

Planning an effective program frequently calls for special methods of collaboration between schools of social work and schools of public administration, health, or agriculture. This sort of collaboration is particularly important for students coming from the so-called underdeveloped countries where all social problems, such as illiteracy, ill-health, bad housing, unemployment, and mass poverty, so obviously run together and must be attacked together. Many of these students will have to take charge of community development programs in their countries. Therefore, it is essential that they learn how to work effectively with those in other professional fields, particularly doctors, teachers, agriculturalists, nutritionists, and engineers. They must know their own field of competence and know the contribution they can make working with these other professional people, either as specialist or generalist, in the sense of integrating, focusing, and making more effective the work of other specialists.

Planning also must include field work experience. This probably is even more essential for these foreign students than for the American students, in order that they may really understand and apply what they have learned in the classroom. I know the schools find the development of field placement opportunities difficult, due to language, different cultural background, frequently different customs in dress, and other factors. Therefore, it is gratifying that it was possible to provide actual field work, and not simply observation, for 86 percent of the foreign students under Social Security Administration sponsorship during the fiscal year 1952–53. However, very few were afforded an opportunity to acquire field experience in group work, community organization, or social administration, although the courses selected by them indicate a large proportion are interested in these areas.

A frequent comment made by these students is that social work in America is too individualistic. While they all laud us for our emphasis on the dignity and worth of the individual, apparently many go home with the impression that we fail to recognize sufficiently the necessity for social legislation and better social organization generally. This impression may be due in part to our failure to call attention to the very substantial body of social legislation that exists in America and in part to our failure to relate case work to social programs carried on under both private and public auspices. In any event, as I shall indicate later, it would be well for us to reflect on this frequent comment in its application to the training not only of these foreign students but also of all students.

I think all along the line we have seen a considerable improvement and refinement in our planning with international visitors. Sponsoring agencies and schools are providing orientation programs better geared to the individual needs of trainees. There is greater emphasis on early orientation to the American community—its institutions and customs. For example, the Social Security Administration has worked out a plan with several communities near Washington to allow groups of from two to five trainees to visit for two weeks of observation under the guidance of an experienced social welfare leader in that community. In addition to visiting the various welfare, health, and education facilities, the trainees also visit farms, stores, factories, labor organizations, and churches. Some of the evenings are spent in American homes, and these are indeed most significant occasions to the international guests. I understand that a number of schools of social work are also planning similar orientation seminars for the period just prior to the student's entrance in a school of social work.

It seems to me that we cannot overemphasize the role of the school adviser or the agency adviser in making the trainee's experience in this country successful. A school taking on responsibility for foreign students needs to make specific provision for extra consultation time with a staff adviser as an essential part of the training program. While we all would hope that the international student can fit into the general framework of the curriculum and planning at the school, experience shows that in most instances there needs to be some individualization, particularly as regards the work load the student can carry, the timing of new experiences, and the selection of courses. Sometimes language presents a problem. In other instances the adjustment to a new cultural setting affects the student's readiness to cope with new learning experience. Let us not forget that, in addition to trying to learn new professional principles and methods, almost every student from another country finds that America presents challenging new philosophical concepts different from those he has taken for granted for most of his life.

We must recognize that our training cannot be geared to particular programs or to the needs of any special groups of countries. However, we can do certain things in this learning experience which will bridge the differences and help the students see how the learning of basic concepts and methods will be helpful in his immediate situation. In the first place, the faculties of the schools can develop a greater awareness of what is happening in these different countries, so that there is a sympathetic understanding of the student's needs. Here in New York they have an unusual opportunity to do so through the Columbia School of International Affairs and because of their proximity to the United Nations and its informed Secretariat. Providing fellowships for faculty members to study social welfare developments abroad and the part that trained social workers play in them is invaluable in this regard. Secondly, they can help the student to realize that, while he will not find a situation "like home" or learn a specific program he can "take home," he will be learning how to work with individuals, with groups, and with the community—and they can also help him realize that experience has demonstrated these new skills can be applied to meet a variety of social needs under many different circumstances.

One of our more experienced trainees, returning to Africa to the job of training social workers for the village, comments:

Native society is still very clannish. The principles of group work can provide a very valuable means of approach to the people of Africa. . . . In this widespread effort to improve the social and economic life of the peasants in the interior of the country, the community is built around a community center. All these centers could be very well termed "settlement houses" in the fullest meaning of the word; the main purpose of those centers being the creation of a community sense and community feeling.

At the University Center, where I will be working after my return to the Belgian Congo, my first and main office will be to teach the natives, coming from all parts of the country, and preparing themselves to return to their own part of the country to take care of those "Social Centers." They will work in close cooperation with the Administration to improve the local communities and to solve the problems of adaptation to the new social and economic conditions.

He also refers to the growing urban centers

where the social worker will not only have to cope with the changing social and economic conditions, but where the mingling of tribes and customs, together with the wreckage of the old traditional society, has to be overcome by the creation of a new social and economic complex based, as much as possible, on the traditional structure and taking in consideration the basic trends of African society. It seems to me that the job which the alumni of the University Centrum will assume is not only important but really vital for the sound development of the African society. They cannot be too well prepared for such a task and the study of the principles of Group Work and Community Organization can be of essential help to the accomplishment of this tremendous task.

The report demonstrates that this trained observer had bridged the gap between his own program needs and what he found in American social work training. He could identify the universal despite the tremendous difference in setting. But it also demonstrates that with the best of efforts on our part the hard fact remains that foreign trainees and observers will need to decide for themselves how much of what they learn is applicable to their own country. Obviously it is impossible to duplicate or even approximate in this country the social setting in which they will need to apply what they have learned here. And we cannot hope that many of the faculty members and agency supervisors will be completely familiar with conditions in the countries from which these trainees come. Therefore, it seems most desirable that study abroad should be increasingly reserved for the experienced worker with the background and maturity to relate principles and methodology to the reality of conditions back home. This fundamental difficulty in providing basic social work training can best be overcome by American social workers assisting in the establishment of schools of social work in the underdeveloped countries themselves. When this is not feasible, it should at least be possible to establish regional training centers to serve a homogeneous area.

It is encouraging to find that interest in developing indigenous training facilities increases as more countries become acquainted with the principles and practices of social work training in the United States. Almost without exception American social work consultants sent to other countries by the United Nations or through a United States program have assisted in establishing or strengthening social work schools or in-service training programs. Likewise, most of the American teachers who have gone to other countries have had to shoulder considerable responsibility in developing field work units. The idea of practice under supervision which is so central to the American teaching of social work has been overlooked in large part in many of these countries. Certain of our consultants report that they have been particularly successful in developing field work experience in group work.

One training consultant writes:

In general the students have responded somewhat more to group activities than to casework activities. In part this is due, it is believed, to the fact that group activities have been less subject to the limitations imposed by the lack of facilitating services available to meet the social problems presented by individuals. Also, the difficulties of providing service outside of an organized agency structure have been greater with respect to the casework practice than with respect to group work.

PREPARING AMERICANS FOR SERVICE ABROAD

Social workers already have a long and significant record of achievement in service abroad. They rendered invaluable service to the military authorities in dealing with the great social problems arising in the battle areas in World War II. They served well the governments in coping with the social aftermath of the war and in the re-establishment of welfare institutions. They served UNRRA in its great work of relief and rehabilitation. They served the International Refugee Organization in the repatriation and resettlement of millions of persons. They are now serving the United Nations and its specialized agencies in many ways and in many parts of the world.

It goes without saying that American social workers who go overseas as welfare advisers, whether to assist in the establishment of training facilities or for some other purpose, ought to have some familiarity with the countries concerned. As I have already suggested, the Columbia School of International Affairs offers an unusual opportunity to social workers to acquire a useful background of knowledge upon which to build through first-hand contact. Moreover, there is a wealth of material coming through United Nations channels and through reports made to official and voluntary agencies by American social workers returning from other countries. Every social worker should be familiar with the report on "The World Social Situation" published by the United Nations Department of Social Affairs in November,

1952. A study of this report will help broaden the perspective of American social workers and stimulate a reconsideration of how social welfare skills can make their maximum contribution toward solving the problems portrayed in so many of the countries of the world. Similarly, in the field of social administration the studies carried out by the United Nations Division of Social Welfare, the International Labor Organization, and other groups describe new and different patterns of social organization for carrying on social programs. If we can introduce this type of material into our curriculum, our training seminars and institutes, we will have made a significant step forward in better preparation for our international responsibilities.

We must remember that American social workers who go abroad will not themselves administer social programs. Rather, they will serve as advisers to national officials who are responsible for social planning and social administration. They will also assist, as I have just suggested, in setting up necessary training programs for both in-school and in-service training. In some instances these in-service programs have been set up for untrained social workers—as beginning preparation for a job in a new social service in the country. However, in many cases, these students later complete their professional training at a school of social work.

The social welfare adviser overseas also finds himself frequently called upon to cooperate in the training programs of technicians in other fields, such as teachers and nurses. Thus a welfare consultant (in Peru) reports on her participation in a workshop on community organization in the Andean communities where she was a discussion leader with a group of teachers from these rural areas. The rural teachers were the only available personnel to take on some basic community organization, and they needed help on how to get started.

Many of the American social workers who have gone abroad have served as advisers in connection with the development of a specialized program. An increasing number are now being asked to assist in the planning and development of general social welfare programs. *But* both the specialized social worker and those who will be assisting in the development of a general social welfare program must have a background that enables them to relate their specific assignment to the total economic and social planning going on in the country or area to which they are assigned. They must understand that most of the drive for technical assistance gets its impetus from a desire to accelerate the economic development of a country or area. They must also realize that too often the assumption is that increased economic development automatically results in increased social welfare.

Of course, there is no disagreement with the belief that the end result of economic development should be improved wellbeing of the people. And improved health conditions and reduction in illiteracy are recognized as necessary companion programs to the strictly economic projects undertaken. But unfortunately the necessity for definite and sustained thought being given to the actual social effects of economic development is not always recognized. Nor is there complete understanding that improved social organization is absolutely necessary as an aid to economic development.

It is therefore essential that social workers going abroad thoroughly understand the many undesirable social effects of the industrial revolution which many countries of the Western world experienced in the last century. Indeed there is hardly a country today that has fully remedied the social evils flowing from rapid economic development. It would be tragic if we permitted history to repeat itself in connection with these great international efforts now being made to promote economic development. But of course it is not sufficient for social welfare advisers merely to raise a warning voice against repetition of the mistakes of the past. They must be prepared to assume a far more affirmative role in promoting the sort of social organization which will not only minimize the social disadvantages of economic development but maximize the social advantages. They must be able to show how effective social organization is an indispensable aid to economic development.

Too often in connection with these international efforts to promote the economic development of countries do we Americans think in terms of great projects to control and take advantage of natural resources. We think in terms of great dams to control floods, furnish electric power, and provide irrigation. We are too prone to think in terms of great industrial undertakings and improved transportation facilities. We oftentimes fail to realize that the carrying out of these great projects will require many years and large capital, to say nothing of the development of the necessary technological skills of the population. We are likely to forget that while these great projects are under way, it is necessary to develop better social organization in all of the little towns and villages and rural areas of a country. As many of the leaders of these underdeveloped countries have said, their greatest resource is the people themselves. And it is only through social organization that this great resource can be effectively utilized.

One of the things which has impressed American consultants most is the conviction of the new governments regarding the welfare of the people. They seldom find opposition on philosophical grounds as regards the government's responsibility toward people. Discussions center around financing, organization, and training of personnel. This philosophy is reflected in the expression of government representatives at international seminars and conferences as they meet to discuss social welfare developments and problems. A representative of Jordan at the recent United Nations Middle East Seminar in Damascus put it in these words in regard to social assistance:

Our aim here is no longer a favor extended by a financially able person to a poor one, or by a philanthropist whenever he likes, so as to exalt his fame; it is a responsibility and a duty which our countries have assumed towards individuals, families or communities as a matter of right which is required in the interest of society, as well as its security and prosperity.

The leaders in these countries realize that this philosophy of government responsibility must be translated into action through sound administration. One of our American social welfare advisers writing from the Middle East observes that the country where he was serving "has only begun to learn the art of government. Most mature people here remember the days when the key bureaucratic jobs were held by foreigners. The last of these left the government less than a decade ago." And this situation is repeated in country after country where new, inexperienced national governments taking over from old imperial powers face the problems of public administration of broad social programs.

Another American adviser, writing again from the Middle East about a new social security program, reports:

The law itself provides a good basis for administration and there is constructive leadership . . . [but] the structure has in a sense still to be created. Personnel needs to be increased—jobs need to be defined and authority and responsibility delegated. A systematic recording of operating and fiscal facts must be developed . . . the usual tools for administration do not exist.

And then, in a more optimistic vein:

This leadership believes in training. In the main, however, they have seen the training as addressed only to beginners—or in the form of

overseas fellowships. The intimate relationship and integration of
in-service training with administration . . . has yet to be recognized. . . . The problems here are of incredible difficulty. One must
think in decades not years. Under any circumstances it takes time to
master the administrative arts. It takes much longer to do this while
overcoming economic obstacles that are the product of a sparse environment and centuries of foreign occupation. It takes still longer
to do this in a country which is in process of reconciling the contributions of East and West, combining them to form a new national
consciousness.

A number of countries have already under way definite programs of community organization and development which show
tangible results and have lifted the hearts of the people. Therefore, it is essential that social welfare advisers be prepared to
assist in the training of community leaders in all of these countries. They must be able to show them how to stimulate community action, how to marshal community resources, and how
to maximize the contribution of specialists from other fields. In
the United States when we think of community organization, we
think too largely in terms of coordinating the activities of many
social agencies already in existence in a community. But in these
underdeveloped countries there are no social agencies to coordinate. Therefore, it is necessary to build from the ground up,
working directly with the people of a community and helping
them to cope with the stark problems of human existence.

This lack of specialized services available in local communities emphasizes the need for training community leaders who
can assess their own situation and work out plans to use regional
or traveling specialists who will serve only as consultants for the
purpose of initiating certain projects but who cannot remain to
assist in their full development. The social worker advising on
these village development programs must be equipped with

some understanding of the simpler measures which communities can take to improve health, literacy, housing, and food production. Where our social work consultants do not already have knowledge and understanding in related fields of public health, nutrition, and education, it is essential that we provide this information as part of their orientation prior to departure for overseas missions.

There is already accumulated a considerable body of experience regarding community organization and development in many parts of the world although it is only two years since the Social Commission of the United Nations recommended that the Division of Social Welfare give high priority to this activity. At that time the development of rural welfare centers in Egypt had come to be rather well known. This development had been so successful that the representatives from underdeveloped countries who were members of the Social Commission were desirous that the United Nations promote a similar development in other countries.

The Division of Social Welfare has assembled a considerable amount of information regarding these developments. In addition, the Division, realizing that the mere collection of information through the questionnaire method would not be sufficient, has conducted a number of surveys and has a number of case studies of these developments.[3] The point has now been reached when on the basis of this general information and these intensive studies it should be possible to develop general principles and a general methodology.

It must be recognized that all these programs—village development programs, social centers, and other broad rural improvement measures—should be regarded as an integral part of local

[3] See, for example, *Social Progress through Local Action*, Study Kit No. 1, 1953. Published jointly by the United Nations and UNESCO.

government administration or appropriately related to it. They can be successful only as they take advantage of local government organization, and they can be of maximum and long-range benefit only as they influence local government administration.

The national government of course must be relied upon to promote and extend community organization throughout the entire country. Therefore, it is of paramount importance that there be in the national government of a country a responsible unit to appraise and apply the developing experience. This unit in the national government should also be responsible for or closely related to national units administering other social programs, such as public assistance and social insurance.

Social welfare has a great opportunity in these countries. It represents a major avenue for democratic contact between people and their government. For those peoples who have known little but colonial administration the new social reforms under their own government take on meaning and significance only as services become tangible in their local community. As countries move from the feudal system of the colonial period to a freer social order, there will be many ways in which the government, acting through its local welfare representatives, can help the community make the adjustment. A local welfare office can and should be the center toward which the community looks for its information, its help in meeting common problems, and its channel for expressing local needs. The office should serve as a continuing expression of the government's concern and interest in the people and their problems. It should provide the security needed when community and family customs are changing. This social welfare service in some countries will take the form of specific services such as public assistance, community centers, recreational facilities, and the like. The important thing is that it gets established as the basic social organization in the local community and serves as the focus both for identifying needs and for helping local groups find a common solution to their problems. Through proper social organization, even on a most limited scale, the government at once expresses its recognition of the importance of the individual and creates the climate so necessary for his development as a responsible participating citizen in the new order.

Besides making an immediate and basic contribution toward the social welfare needs of the community, the welfare organization, if properly staffed with personnel well oriented to allied services, can facilitate the introduction and more efficient use of technical aid in various fields such as health and food production. In the large rural areas where specialized service is so scarce, there is little time for each specialist to create his own community organization. The social worker can assist the community in finding and using specialist assistance for meeting its problems. He can ensure that the community learns to work together on common needs through methods democratically arrived at. The social worker, among all the professions, has learned to "start where the community is." He is skilled in helping the community decide when it is ready to move.

The greatest asset social workers can have as advisers to these countries is a real sense of proportion. They must bring from the outside objectivity in assessing the situation and experience in what will produce the best results with limited resources. They must have a sense of priority, putting first things first, realizing that they cannot accomplish everything that needs to be accomplished. They must be prepared to take full advantage of what in this country they would consider "untrained workers" and "volunteers." Indeed they must proceed upon the assumption that so-called untrained workers and volunteers will be their most precious asset.

In serving as advisers to local and national government officials, social workers will be called upon to advise not only regarding methodology but also regarding social policy. Therefore, it is most important that social workers have a clear understanding of their responsibility in the field of social policy. It is even more important in the international field than in the domestic field that social workers distinguish between whatever personal views they may have regarding social policy and the contribution that they can make based upon their particular professional competence.

It is well known that in this country social workers are criticized from within the profession for not being more interested and active in promoting social policy, or what is usually referred to as "social action." At the same time they are criticized from without the profession for being too prone to participate in any movement or cause alleged to have a social objective, regardless of the validity of the approach and regardless of whether they are in a position to make a professional contribution.

As I understand the use of the term "social action," it covers a range of activity, including the development of administrative policy under existing social legislation, the improvement of existing social legislation, and the enactment of additional social legislation as well as social reform directed toward fundamental changes in existing institutions. As one moves from the development of administrative policy under existing social legislation toward social reform directed to achieving fundamental changes in existing institutions, it becomes increasingly important as well as increasingly difficult to determine the extent to which social workers should participate in their professional capacity rather than in their individual capacity as citizens. Therefore, when they are called upon to serve as advisers to a foreign government, they must be very certain that they do not transcend their responsibility as technical advisers and thus infringe upon the responsibility of government officials regarding any necessary social reforms. Social workers can be of maximum usefulness in the development of sound social policy in other countries by confining their role to that of making available to the policy-makers their professional knowledge and understanding of social needs and the problems involved in meeting these needs. They can and should, of course, assist the policy-makers in their consideration of possible alternative ways and means of achieving indigenously determined social objectives. To go beyond this would be to run the risk of destroying their usefulness as technical advisers.

As these new governments find their bearings and get under way, the social welfare adviser must be prepared for political upsets. Overnight the gains of months and years may seem lost. Therefore, the adviser, in addition to maintaining his own courage, must bolster the courage of the social workers of the country concerned. An experienced American consultant writes:

The instability of the government in the country is of course both a result and a cause of the way things are done. Everything has been so mixed up with the rapidly changing political situation; the people feel at the same time a necessity to "make hay while the sun shines" and a futility about the transition aspect of anything they may get done. . . . Leadership is very, very individual, and the removal of one person . . . can change the course of happenings for hundreds of people. There is instability of organization, as yet. However, I want to close on a hopeful note, on the note of the excellent leadership that does exist, on the note of an encouraging number of our students (at the school of social service) who are not only going to be good social workers but people with vision and perspective and what here is called "emocion social."

SOME BASIC PROBLEMS INVOLVED
IN ALL SOCIAL WORK EDUCATION

While it is true that we are confronted with special problems in training social workers so that they may function effectively in the field of international social welfare activities, I think that for the most part we really are confronted with the same fundamental problems involved in training social workers so that they may function effectively right here at home.

First of all we must come to grips with the question of just what are (or should be) the universal characteristics of social work as a profession—what has been called the common core of social work. I need not stress the fact that the basic philosophy underlying social work is an abiding and indestructible belief in the dignity and the worth of every human being. From this fundamental belief flows not only our belief in the brotherhood of man but our belief that human beings have a right to be different and have a right to manage their own affairs. It would be presumptuous to assert that this fundamental belief is the exclusive possession of social workers. But it would also be wrong not to recognize that this belief constitutes the bedrock upon which the practice of social work is and must be based.

Donald Howard has suggested the following definition of social work:

Generally speaking, social work in any country is that discipline, distinguished by a characteristic synthesis of philosophy and knowledge, attitudes and skills, whose primary responsibility is to assist entire societies, communities, groups and individuals to attain for themselves the highest possible level of well-being but which, when necessary, is responsible for supplying (directly or indirectly) the goods and services essential to the welfare of the individuals and communities concerned.[4]

The Hollis-Taylor report criticizes such a definition, as follows: "To say that the profession is concerned with helping people to make the most effective and satisfying use of themselves and of the society in which they live is either to make a social worker out of every person of good will, or to claim for the social worker a universality of technical knowledge, which he would be the first to disclaim." Similarly, the report criticizes the attempt to characterize social work in terms of its basic philosophy and points out that "belief in democracy as a way of life and a conviction of the dignity and the importance of the individual are not peculiar to social workers." [5] But the report does agree that these broad claims give a clue to the essential contributions of professional social work, namely, that while the social worker relies upon the findings of the social and biological sciences, in making use of these findings he does so on the basis of a value judgment which stresses the importance of the individual.

Gordon Hamilton puts it this way: "Within social work's distinctive method I have placed first the bringing together of ethics with the knowledge and disciplines of science." [6] To my way of thinking, this is the glory and the strength of social work, especially in a world that is so rampant with suspicion, hatred, conflict, and exploitation.

[4] Donald S. Howard, "The Common Core of Social Work in Different Countries," in *The Social Welfare Forum*, Official Proceedings of the National Conference of Social Work, 1951 (New York, Columbia University Press, 1951), p. 26.

[5] Ernest V. Hollis, and Alice L. Taylor, *Social Work Education in the United States; the Report of a Study Made for the National Council on Social Work Education* (New York, Columbia University Press, 1951), p. 114.

[6] Gordon Hamilton, "The Role of Social Casework in Social Policy," *Social Casework*, October, 1952, p. 317.

But if the social work profession is to achieve its high purpose, it can do this only through social workers who are not only aware of that high purpose but who also possess the necessary knowledge and skills to translate that purpose into action. I think there is general agreement that social workers should first of all have acquired an education rich in the humanities, the social sciences, and the natural sciences; that is, an education which opens the door to an understanding of the biological, social, and spiritual nature of mankind. Most, if not all, of this basic education should be obtained as an undergraduate, but I believe it is of paramount importance that it should be recognized and organized as an integral part of professional education, just as in the fields of law and medicine.

When we turn to graduate professional education in social work, as I see it, there is considerable disagreement as to emphasis, degree of specialization, and interrelationship of subjects taught, but considerable agreement as to the general character of such education. The statement on curriculum policy issued in May, 1952, by the American Association of Schools of Social Work (now the Council on Social Work Education) set a broad framework for social work education which might well be used internationally. Regarding the curriculum as "a cohesive whole," the statement outlines the major areas for the total curriculum and suggests the concept of a broad generic approach in teaching. It recommends that

the social work curriculum should provide, through classroom and field instruction and through research, knowledge and understanding of the social services, their development, their relation to the social order, to social change, and to the needs of people; knowledge and understanding of human behavior, needs and aspirations; and knowledge and understanding of social work practice. . . . Provision should be made for all students to receive an introduction to the common objectives, principles, and methods, as well as to the unique elements, of social case work, social group work, community organization in social work, administration in social work, and research in social work. Class and field instructors should be prepared to identify the professional skills that are common to all social work practice and to assist the student to develop an awareness of how these common skills are utilized in all social work practice.

The progress we have made in identifying the common core of professional knowledge and skill has particular significance for the international field. As I see it, the further we advance toward identifying the generic, the nearer we come to identifying what is truly universal. In other words, the more we clarify for American social work the concepts and methods that are common to social work in a variety of settings in America, the more clearly we see what can be taught and found useful in any setting anywhere throughout the world.

It would obviously be presumptuous for me to attempt to tell social work educators how to construct the curriculum of a particular school to achieve this objective. They know, far better than I do, the limitations within which they must function in terms of money, time, faculty, characteristics of the student body, and demands of social welfare agencies. However, I would like to say something about my reaction to the current discussions going on relative to curriculum.

One of the basic questions is the relationship of case work to other phases of social work. Perhaps I should say rather that the basic question is whether case work is synonomous with social work. This has been a burning question for a long time. It is contended that case work teaching emphasizes too much the psychoanalytical and psychiatric approach, fails to recognize sufficiently the importance of environmental forces, and does not recognize and apply knowledge and skills which are common to individual case work, group work, and community organization. It is also contended that the teaching of case work is not properly related to the teaching of other subjects, that a disproportionate time is devoted to case work and that it is taught too dogmatically. But I think we can all agree with the statement that "casework has been the matrix out of which most social work principles, content, and processes have emerged." Therefore, should we not direct our attention more affirmatively to a consideration of how these principles, content, and processes can best contribute to what is now being called the generic social work method, described by Arlien Johnson as "that necessary body of knowledge, principles, and skills which enable a social worker to offer constructive, purposive service through social welfare agencies to individuals, groups and communities." [7]

The Hollis-Taylor report contains this challenging statement:

This report also rejects the idea widely held by social workers that casework, group work, and community organization are social work specializations. In reality, they are major areas of curriculum which, by analogy, bear a relation to the whole social work curriculum similar to that which the humanities, the natural sciences, and the social sciences as groups bear to the whole undergraduate or graduate curriculum in arts and sciences. Even a cursory examination of the professional functions which social work specialists perform, leads to the conclusion that all of them need to drink deeply at these three springs of professional learning. [8]

I think there is now general recognition of the essential unity of case work, group work, community organization, and social policy. But the problem remains of spelling out just exactly what should be included in generic social work method and developing a curriculum accordingly. In addition, there is the equally crucial

[7] Arlien Johnson, "The Hollis-Taylor Report as Seen from the Viewpoint of a Social Work Educator," *Social Work Journal*, July, 1952, pp. 132–37.

[8] Hollis and Taylor, *op. cit.*, p. 251.

problem of actually applying the philosophy, concepts, and techniques of generic social work method to a broad field of practice.

Besides calling attention to this community of interests, so to speak, between case work, group work, and community organization, I should like to comment upon the relationship between case work on the one hand and social policy on the other. Social work, a child of the social sciences, should maintain at all costs its social orientation and its awareness of the importance of the environmental situation in which individuals must live as social beings. In the development of its own special methods, social work must not sacrifice anything by way of breadth of training. While that has been far more characteristic of other professions than of social work, by its very nature social work should be especially aware of the importance of social factors in promoting the well-being of individuals. Of course there is no necessary conflict or dichotomy or even dualism in the individual and social approaches. I believe that through the proper development of social work we can and must help close the gap between the individual and the social approach.

No one has more persuasively urged that social work should effectively relate these two essentially complementary approaches than Gordon Hamilton. She has truly said that "one cannot successfully solve problems of inter-relationships without a sound economic and political structure, but it is also true that one cannot solve—and this is less readily granted—economic problems without profound understanding of human behavior." She has pointed out that "the strength of social work lies in its ability to operate at both ends of the psychosocial event, in its refusal to limit itself either to the manipulation of external factors alone, even though this is one of its traditional and proper concerns, or to the treatment of inner factors alone even though the latter have been vastly tempting." She goes on to say that "there are those who urge social workers to become community organizers and administrators, but do not yet realize that an adequate concept of personality and behavior is as essential to sound legislation, to programs, to institutions and to administration, as it is in treatment." [9]

It is important that the scope of social work training and practice in this country should be devoted in a much greater degree to the development and execution of general social programs. Otherwise we will continue to find that the persons most active in shaping and administering these large-scale programs will be trained in other professions, such as law, economics, and public administration, or will acquire such training as they possess in a purely pragmatic manner. However, we will not solve the problem by simply adding to the curriculum courses in public welfare, social administration, and social research. Certainly we increase the problem if we continue to add courses to train for an increasing number of special settings.

Is it not rather obvious that the solution lies in applying our evolving generic social work method more largely to general social programs, such as the organization of whole communities (not simply community chests and councils) and the development of public assistance, social insurance, and constructive social services which should be made available to all members of a community? Will it not also be necessary to depend more largely upon field practice and in-service training for the application of general training to specific settings? I need hardly add that this calls for effective two-way cooperation between the schools and the social agencies, especially the governmental agencies, which have been particularly concerned about the suitability of training to meet their needs.

[9] Hamilton, *op. cit.*, pp. 317–21.

In our efforts to clarify and apply our ideas regarding generic social work method, let us not forget the importance of devoting enough attention to research, so that social workers are made aware of the value of research in acquiring an understanding of social problems and how to cope with them. Indeed, I would say that "research-mindedness" is a test of the stage of development of a profession.

It should be rather obvious that research is essential in planning and appraising a welfare program, whether it be a local, state, or national program, and whether it be governmental or nongovernmental. But the value of research as a continuing aid to effective day-to-day administration is often overlooked. Too often practitioners and administrators become so engrossed or beset by their manifold duties and problems that they fail to realize the help they can get from properly organized research related to practice. But properly planned research is necessary for testing principles and generalizations upon which practice proceeds. Social workers, trained as they are in the careful recording of information, are in an exceptionally advantageous position to supply data and to formulate questions as a basis for effective research.

Every practitioner and every researcher should be aware of this complementary character of his respective function, and every administrator should make certain that the "feed-back" principle is applied in his organization; that is, research should take full advantage of the data growing out of practice and practice should take full advantage of research findings. I need hardly add that training in research is of particular value to both the welfare advisers who go abroad and to our friends from abroad who come here for training. As pioneers, they will need to assemble and analyze material for the construction, development, and continuing appraisal of the new social programs for which they are responsible.

I have devoted so much attention to these fundamental questions concerning social work training in general because, as I have already indicated, I believe that the extent to which we are able to train social workers to function effectively here at home determines the extent to which we are able to meet our responsibilities for training in the field of international social welfare.

THE CHALLENGE TO
SOCIAL WORK EDUCATORS

I realize that I have outlined a difficult role for social work educators in this country and for social work advisers who go abroad. But I know from personal knowledge that social work advisers and social work educators have already made a tremendous contribution in the field of international social welfare; and this is particularly true of the faculty and graduates of the New York School of Social Work. The comments made by hundreds of trainees regarding what they have learned by way of the philosophy, concept, and practice of social work in this country are in themselves a most eloquent testimony to the great contribution that social work educators have made.

I am sure, too, that we are all aware that at the same time that we are attempting to make a contribution in the field of international social welfare, our visitors from abroad are making a great contribution to social work in this country. We have again discovered that there is nothing so illuminating as to see ourselves as others see us. They have caused us to re-examine and reappraise much to which we have become habituated. They have helped us in our search for the solid core of social work and in the development of generic social work method. They have made us realize that we must give more attention to social forces and factors. They have pointed up the need for training for large-scale social programs. They have shown us the need for a less segmented approach toward social welfare. They have emphasized the need for closer collaboration between public and voluntary agencies and the need for giving attention to the common elements in public assistance and social insurance. In other words, they have brought us to a better realization that we must give attention not only to the whole person but to the whole community in the largest sense of the term.

It is of the very nature of the social work profession to be constantly appraising the social contribution that it is making as a profession. This is as it should be. Every profession should engage in this constant self-appraisal. But there is a difference between being aware of the possibility of further progress in the profession and being unduly apologetic as regards the progress that has already been made. We need not be embarrassed because we are unable to establish the exact metes and bounds of what constitutes the social work profession. Other far older professions are still uncertain as to their metes and bounds. And interestingly enough, these older professions, such as law and medicine, are now finding the need for giving attention to the social aspects of their respective professions. Indeed, they have discovered the need for enlisting the services of social workers in the practice of their professions.

The humanitarian justification for social welfare activities is of course supreme and is justification in itself. But social workers have an obligation to promote social welfare activities as an integral phase of the dynamics of social progress. I emphasize this because in a low-level economy with poverty, sickness, illiteracy, and misery affecting the entire population instead of only relatively few individuals, it is necessary for social welfare to seek its justification in the advancement of the total population.

The great strength of social work in promoting the welfare of the total population is its faith in and reliance upon the fundamental principles of democracy. Social workers not only believe in the worth of every single human being but also believe in the infinite perfectability of human beings and in their ability to cooperate with each other in an ever widening sphere. They believe, with Woodrow Wilson, that the highest efficiency is the willing cooperation of a free people. And while social workers would be the first to disclaim a monopoly in the understanding of human needs and human motivations, they can rightly claim a more intensive and sustained interest in utilizing human knowledge and human institutions to promote social well-being. They have at all times and in many ways emphasized that all human activities and institutions begin with and end with individual human beings.

Eventually democracy is bound to achieve its goal of equality of opportunity everywhere. I firmly believe that this century which now seems so tragic will be known in ages to come as the century in which the democratic ideal first captured the imagination of the entire world. I also believe that in a very real sense social work is the handmaiden of democracy in its world-wide march.

PEACE, FREEDOM, AND

SOCIAL WELFARE

I MUST at the outset qualify myself as an amateur in the field of
social work. The experience on which this paper is based is a
period of five years' service in government which brought me into
almost daily contact with the United Nations in the formative years 1947–52, during which it became clear that the young
world organization was not to be allowed to fulfill quickly and
easily the high promise of 1945. I have, in this paper, directed my
attention to the relation between international action in the
social field and the maintenance of peace, in order that the
reader might have the impressions of one who has been preoccupied with political and security matters and only indirectly
with social action.

If kaleidoscopic impressions are to convey meaning, some background is required, but the scene is turbulent and complex and
forces us to a few brief strokes of oversimplification.

As we enter the second half of the twentieth century the
paramount security issue before mankind is the threat of World
War III. In a sense, this is a more limited concern than the more
general problem of maintaining international peace. A condition
of complete tranquillity is not the only alternative to World War
III. To reverse the statement, we do not have to suppose that

any outbreak of violence necessarily leads to general war. Clashes between Jew and Arab, between Indian and Pakistani, and between Dutch and Indonesian are problems of peace, but perhaps not of World War III. Other acts of violence in Greece, Berlin, or Korea, on the other hand, are intimately and dangerously related to general war. The difference lies in what is behind the violence, whether the breach of the peace is over local and limited issues or a part of a course of conduct which can be developed as a threat to the entire world community. Keeping the peace involves two quite separate tasks, the one to resolve differences among those who fundamentally accept the basic assumptions and rules of an international society, the other to prevent the destruction of that society by those whose purposes are incompatible with it. The role of cooperative action in the social field may be quite different in the two situations. It may exert a powerful and constructive influence for peace among those who are joined in common purposes without being able to bridge the gaps where such purposes are absent.

That World War III is our most ominous public issue, there would seem to be little doubt. Armaments to prevent it or to win it are absorbing vast quantities of mankind's limited physical resources. Its shadow distorts and complicates the solution of many problems which could be resolved by reason and mutual accommodation in another climate. Fear and anxiety lead to suspicion and hostility not only between confessed rivals but among those who ought to be friends. Resources which are desperately needed for the improvement of standards of living are, of necessity, invested in essential security. Under the shadow of World War III, our own democratic processes show signs of stress as the cohesion and mutual confidence of our citizens are weakened by suspicion and uncertainty. The life planning of our young people, the pursuit of scholarship and science, the enjoyment of the arts, the exchange of ideas across national frontiers are directly affected by the threat of war. In fact, the destructiveness of World War III is already being felt, in advance of any military phase of the conflict itself. Our present task is a dual one—to prevent the outbreak of the military phase and to reduce as we can the destructive effects we are already feeling.

General and total war transcends the historical problem of maintaining peace. Atomic and hydrogen weapons pose literally the issue of human survival. Quite apart from such "ultimate" weapons, the increasing violence of warfare by conventional means suggests the possibility that large-scale warfare has developed inner contradictions which destroy its usefulness for achieving any rational purpose. For example, American military leadership in World War II has been criticized in some quarters for not having fought the war in relation to a planned postwar political pattern, for not having employed military means to bring about a more advantageous political consequence. I venture to suggest that our military leaders strove for the speediest possible conclusion of the fighting for an underlying political purpose of the first importance—to get the war over with before the basic institutions of civilization melted away. The urgency of military action was spurred by the observable disintegration of the economic, intellectual, cultural, and moral framework of civilized life. The fighting had to end before it became impossible to sustain it and while there was something left on which to rebuild a tolerable society. This cannot, of course, be presented as a firm conclusion of fact but as a suggestion for historical examination.

After the cruel bloodletting and physical destruction of World War II, man almost succeeded in bringing about, in the United Nations, the realization of one of his most cherished dreams— the organization of a durable peace. If we are disappointed that the United Nations has not accomplished in full its crucial task of maintaining the peace, we can draw hope from the fact that its failure was a near miss—only one rogue government systematically blocked its path. This refusal of one major power to conform its conduct to the commonly agreed international standard has cost the rest of the world many tens of billions of dollars and many thousands of lives, the frustration of the hope and promise of the new nations recently appearing on the world scene, and unfortunate diversion from the peaceful pursuits which are high in the hearts of ordinary men and women in all parts of the world.

The international standard of conduct is, in essence, very simple. It is to be found in paragraphs 3 and 4 of Article 2 of the Charter of the United Nations:

3. All Members shall settle their international disputes by peaceful means in such a manner that international peace and security, and justice, are not endangered.

4. All Members shall refrain in their international relations from the threat or use of force against the territorial integrity or political independence of any state, or any other manner inconsistent with the Purposes of the United Nations.

Underlying this standard of conduct is the premise that international society shall consist of a system of independent states conforming their action to the agreed standard. This in turn implies agreement as to which are the states to be considered independent members of the international community. It should not be surprising that it is hard to find solutions to current political issues if the conduct of states betrays a lack of agreement on the fundamental premises of an international society.

When we speak of a world community, we rightly think of the United Nations. Yet we need to be aware of an important qualification in identifying the United Nations with a world community. A community requires something in common besides a signature formally attached to a piece of paper. If other factors making for a community are not present, the signature is illusory. It is hard to see how genuine membership in a world community can rest upon anything less than (a) agreement as to the basic organizational structure of the community itself, (b) agreement to settle international disputes by peaceful means, and (c) agreement not to use force or the threat of force against the other members of the community. As we shall see later, community ought to mean a great deal more; the present point is that it cannot mean less. Nor do we need to require perfection; mistakes will be made, violence will occur, passion will lead to the breach of general rules, stubborn differences may yield slowly and painfully to peaceful processes. But what is essential is an underlying commitment of policy and action, an attitude and habit of conduct which make membership tolerable to the community as a whole.

The United Nations now has 60 members, 58 if we count the fact that the Soviet Union has three memberships. Of these 58, 55 can be counted as bona fide members of the world community on the basis of a demonstrated agreement upon the essentials; 3 have left themselves on the outside through unwillingness to accept in practice the basic rules. Outside the formal framework of the United Nations are some 21 nations generally recognized by other states. Of these, 16 appear to accept the basic requirements of international life and 5 maintain, perhaps under coercion, the attitude of the Soviet Union. Setting aside the accidents of formal membership in the United Nations, there now appear to be some 71 members of an emerging world community, of which the United Nations is the most general representative, and 8 who hold themselves outside. If we speak of the United Nations as a world community, and think of a reasonable commitment to the principles of the Charter rather than mere signatures, we might occasionally remind ourselves that we are speaking of 71 members, some of whom are not official members of the organization. If we recognize that there is an outlaw group outside the world community, it is an incidental fact that certain ones of this outlaw band, including its leader, happen to hold formal membership in the United Nations.

The term "outlaw" is used with some reluctance but with the belief that it helps to portray the true position. For the Soviet Union and its satellites are under a self-imposed banishment from the world community—outlaws because they refuse to accept the continuing invitation to come within the general system of lawful conduct. We are accustomed to think of the chasm thus indicated as a wide one, but we have probably underestimated its depth. To understand it better is to be better prepared to deal with its implications. We would no longer be surprised when outlaws act like outlaws; we would not rely upon unreliable agreements; we would not have our vision or our judgment confused at moments of danger by chagrin or indignation because outlaws do not act like law-abiding citizens. More important, we would see that the sharpest differences between friends in the world community do not compare in gravity with the slightest incident or differences involving outlaw nations. Lastly, we could never be complacent or indifferent about the fact that the outlaws have in their possession atomic weapons and the capacity to deliver them.

What does international action in the social field have to do with the complex political and security issues which claim so much of public attention? Some people must feel that social, economic, humanitarian, and cultural affairs have been treated as the stepchildren of politics. Public interest is aroused by what is little more than a personal skirmish in the Security Council, as when Sir Gladwyn Jebb became a television hero while crossing swords with Mr. Jacob Malik throughout the month of August, 1950. When the General Assembly is in session, the political committees are the main attraction; the economic, social, trusteeship, administrative, and legal committees make little news.

Relatively unknown is the work of the Economic and Social Council and its several commissions and subcommissions; similarly unnoticed is the work of the Specialized Agencies. Who knows that more than 60 million children and mothers in more than seventy-two countries received welfare, health, and nutritional aid in 1952 under United Nations auspices? Who but a small professional audience is aware of the Economic Commission for Europe or of the International Law Commission?

Whatever the reasons, threats to the peace are more absorbing than quiet and patient efforts to remove the causes of war. Social action in the international field lacks the drama of turbulent discord and, consequently, the support which comes from public understanding and interest. This may help to explain why the United States could spend approximately $40 billion for defense in the fiscal year 1952 and, in the autumn of 1952, make strenuous efforts to reduce its contribution to the United Nations by a sum amounting to roughly 1/20,000 of its defense expenditure.

I refer broadly to social action in the international field rather than to the fields encompassed by the professional boundaries of what is called "social work." For my purposes, I begin from the Charter of the United Nations, where we read, extracting from the Preamble,

We the peoples of the United Nations determined . . . to promote social progress and better standards of life in larger freedom, and

For these ends . . . to employ international machinery for the

promotion of the economic and social advancement of all peoples,
Have resolved to combine our efforts to accomplish these aims.

And again, in Article 55:

> . . . the United Nations shall promote:
> a. higher standards of living, full employment, and conditions of
>   economic and social progress and development;
> b. solutions of international economic, social, health, and related
>   problems; and international cultural and educational coopera-
>   tion; and
> c. universal respect for, and observance of, human rights and
>   fundamental freedoms for all without distinction as to race,
>   sex, language or religion.

The social interests and activities of the United Nations are
only a part of the vast field of international social action. We
must include action by governments outside the framework of
the United Nations; the flow of students, teachers, technicians,
and ideas; the work of private philanthropy, whether organized
or on an individual basis; the social and humanitarian activities
of the churches, of schools and colleges, of civic organizations.
International social action is, fortunately, marked by great diversity in purpose, method, organization, and financial support.

My purpose is to invite attention to some of the important by-
products of social action in the world community, rather than
to try to speak of its direct and well-recognized results. This is
not to minimize the vast and constructive accomplishment which
is marked out by specific and tangible benefits to hundreds of
millions of peoples in all parts of the world. Improved sanitation,
better maternal and child care, more and better food, better
working conditions, the attack on illiteracy, narcotics control,
population studies, better housing, the attempts to understand
and reduce the stubborn prejudices which flow from racial and

religious differences, greater understanding across cultural frontiers, increasing awareness of the claims of women to a respected
status and widening opportunity, improvements in standards of
living, a broadening of the concept of public service, the strengthening of individual human rights—these are matters of the
greatest significance in themselves and deserve our interest and
support.

But what does this impressive activity in the social field mean
to the politics of peace?

In the first place, cooperative international action in the social
field will help us to discover the common moral values and aspirations which go into the making of a genuine world community.
The Charter of the United Nations starts with the phrase "We
the peoples of the United Nations." To what extent are "We
the peoples" speaking in the Charter? A glance through the
Preamble shows some imposing phrases—"to reaffirm faith in
fundamental human rights," "the dignity and worth of the
human person," "equal rights of men and women," "justice,"
"social progress," "larger freedom," "tolerance," "good neigh-
bors," "common interest." To what extent do these challenging
phrases represent ideas which are shared as between America
and Europe, Europe and the Middle East, America and South
Asia? Or as among Christian, Muslim, Buddhist, Jew?

The answers go beyond the interest of the philosopher to im-
press themselves upon a wide range of very practical problems.
Do technical assistance programs, for example, rest upon a deep
desire to improve one's standard of living as a step toward a more
worthy human existence? Or does material betterment play a
minor role among the aims of those to whom such programs are
directed? Are there other and more complex values which lie
beneath the words of the Charter upon which joint action in a
world community must rest, such as a respect for God, deeply

rooted impulses toward personal power or personal gain, or a yearning to multiply and prolong human life?

I doubt that we shall fully consolidate a world community of peaceful peoples until we have better answers to such questions than we now have. One suspects, however, that the answers are coming little by little from the men and women who are breaking through the barriers of race, language, religion, and nationality and are turning their hands to modest but specific common tasks. Those who are familiar with the activities of the Economic and Social Council and of the Specialized Agencies know that the list of such common tasks which have been taken up under United Nations auspices is a long and richly diverse one. Whether the object is to repel a sudden outbreak of plague in Egypt, the feeding of undernourished children, the care of Arab refugees, the development of higher-yielding varieties of rice, instruction in maternal care, or air-sea rescue—the common denominator in all such effort is an increase of understanding across cultural and national barriers.

By working at the critical points of human misery and personal conflict, we are learning a great deal about human aspiration; about which things bind us together and which drive us apart; about which spiritual and physical hungers can be satisfied in abundance and which are strife-producing because of the scarcity of supply. But the work itself gives life to the phrase "We the peoples of the United Nations," gives substance to such phrases as "social progress," and gives strength and vitality to the world community.

During my years in government I attended many meetings of the United Nations, particularly of the General Assembly and the Security Council, where representatives were gathered from around the world to deal with hundreds of items of common interest. Issues and personalities change, but running through the debates was a sense of common purpose and a common destiny, ill-defined and largely unspoken, but always present. For lack of a better way of expressing themselves, most representatives turn to the Charter and use its words to try to say what they mean. I have never heard any delegate, not even one from the Soviet Union, speak scornfully of the Charter itself. One suspects that this is not mere accident, that somewhere in the Charter are hidden profound moral values which command general respect. If Mr. Vishinsky was wary about involving the Charter in his cynicism, it was an impressive left-handed tribute, by a skilled propagandist, to the ideas inscribed there. At a minimum, it is an interesting acknowledgment of their strength. My guess is, therefore, that as we probe by international action in the social field into the spiritual and moral stuff of the world community, we shall discover that man, as a human being, is much the same as his fellows and that the activities of the United Nations are founded upon the spiritual and physical needs embedded in his nature.

A second by-product of international action in the social field is the fact that we thereby move beyond the Cold War and establish a basis for our relations with other peoples more deeply rooted and more lasting than the rivalries and controversies of our particular day.

Power relationships are subject to frequent change; there have been four or five major shifts in world power alignments within our own generation. As the consolidation of the great free world coalition goes forward, the distribution of political and military power is now changing once more, thus far without a general conflict. It need not be supposed that the Cold War is a permanent part of our landscape—change is certain, even though it can be for better or for worse.

Whether we like it or not, there are peoples and governments who do not consider themselves directly involved in the Cold War. Some of these are new nations, assuming in recent years full responsibility for their own affairs for the first time in centuries. In this formative and sensitive period, they are gathering and hardening opinions about the rest of us which may last a long time. While most of them are ready to enter into friendly association with us, they are not willing to become pawns in the Cold War. They want our respect for what they are and resent the suggestion that their role is to fit snugly into their assigned spot, a spot determined by our relations with the Soviet Union. It will take time for some of them to see that the threat of aggression is a threat to them, that we want nothing from them for ourselves but some assurance that they will be able to live in peace.

We need not apologize for trying to form a great coalition among peace-loving nations to guarantee our common security. But it is important for us to find a way to tell some of our friends that that is not the whole story. Again, by working with them toward social progress, day by day and task by task, there will emerge a growing recognition that the American people share the hopes and faiths of men and women in other parts of the world.

A third by-product is closely related to the second. By cooperative international action in the social field, we build in fact a unity in the world community which will produce decisive strength at moments of great danger. Although the great majority of the members of the free world are already bound together, by direct agreement or by the inevitable progression of events, under the proposition that an attack on one is an attack on all, the coalition is not complete. If some of those who still remain outside were to be asked today to make a final choice, they would be unwilling or unable to make it and it would be unwise to press them to do so. Preoccupation with their own troubles, their own domestic opinion, and differences in assessing the issues before the world community bar the path to specific and conscious action.

At the same time, these nations are joined with the rest of us in hundreds of meetings throughout the year, searching for agreed answers to thousands of items on the agenda. They are taking part in a wide range of action to improve the lot of their peoples and to give body and substance to the words of the Charter. Little by little, by imperceptible stages, the free community is forming; stone by stone the structure of security is being raised; at moments of danger the strength of the community will be felt because the basic decisions will have already been made.

We had a glimpse of this process on the weekend of the outbreak of the Korean aggression in June, 1950. During those days of breathless suspense in which the world awaited the decision of the United States, one had the impression that there were no neutrals and that the world community had been quickened by danger into a fundamental unity. True, after the decision was made and the danger appeared in fact to be less than feared, the sense of community weakened and other preoccupations reasserted themselves. But it seemed clear on June 27, 1950, that the strength of the United States and its allies was felt to be a force for peace and not an instrument for carrying out selfish ambitions. If this is a correct view, much of the explanation lies with the effort made by this country and its citizens to join with others to repair the damage of war, to deal with hunger, disease, and misery, to teach and to learn across national frontiers, and to work actively with other peoples to get at the great social problems which concern mankind.

A fourth by-product of social action is that we thereby develop habits, procedures, and machinery for dealing with potentially explosive economic and social problems by peaceful means. Were there no Soviet Union and no Cold War, the prospect for peace would then turn upon our capacity to deal amicably with complex economic and social issues which are even now with us, even though somewhat in the background of public interest. Population pressures upon limited foodstuffs in Asia, the trade requirements of thickly populated industrial areas such as Britain, Japan, and western Europe, access to raw materials and to the resources of the great ocean areas, racial and colonial issues are sources of trouble quite apart from the Cold War. In the past, these have been primary causes of international conflict. They furnish differences which Communism can exploit and which may be considered by the Soviet Union as a means for bringing about the eventual collapse of the great community now forming.

By international action in the economic and social field, we are able to face these issues on the assumption that they must be settled by peaceful means, by intelligence, and by a measure of patience and mutual accommodation. We Americans have a vital stake in this matter. For example, the Paley Report tells us that in 1950 we were consuming more basic raw materials than we were producing (a deficiency of 9 percent).[1] The same report indicates that this deficiency in raw materials may reach 20 percent during the decade 1970–80 if our standard of living is to continue to rise. We can meet our own needs only by calling large quantities of raw materials forward from other nations through the channels of trade. At the same time, our American standard of living is substantially higher than that of the major raw material producing areas; it has been estimated that the United States per capita income is about twenty-five times that

[1] *Report of the President's Materials Policy Commission* (Washington, D.C., 1952), I, 2.

of India. It should be apparent that it will not be easy for us to obtain from others over a long period the materials we require to maintain high standards if living standards elsewhere are unbearably low. Pressures on the terms of trade can be expected and are a potential source of discord; no nation has a larger stake than we do in resolving such issues on the basis of peaceful process.

The Paley Commission offered as one of three fundamental concepts the belief that

the destinies of the United States and the rest of the free non-Communist world are inextricably bound together. This belief we hope will color everything we have to say about the Materials Problem. It implies, for example, that if the United States is to increase its imports of materials it must return in other forms strength for strength to match what it receives. It is the Commission's belief that if we fail to work for a rise in the standard of living of the rest of the free world, we thereby hamper and impede the further rise of our own, and equally lessen the chances of democracy to prosper and peace to reign the world over.[2]

A fifth by-product is the opportunity to share some of the crushing responsibility which has fallen to the United States since World War II. We need not recount in detail the serious demands being made upon our resources, our leadership, and our competence. The burden is heavy—and sometimes appears to be unendurable to a people who had not prepared themselves for it. In many of the social fields, however, we find that other governments and peoples are making important contributions, in material resources, in trained manpower, and, even more important, in broadening the base of knowledge and understanding which are also in short supply. If there are seventy-one members of what I have been referring to as the world community, there are vast opportunities for contributions from the

[2] *Ibid.*, p. 3.

other seventy; it is not necessary for the United States to be the senior partner in every such enterprise. In fact, others are contributing on a scale much greater than we in the United States generally understand. Much of this effort is channeled through the United Nations, but the Colombo Plan, colonial development schemes, and the tens of thousands of students in training outside their own countries reflect the diversity of effort being made by others. This type of initiative and good neighborliness on the part of other members of the world community deserves more attention than it gets from Americans, preoccupied with their own burdens. Incidentally, from the point of view of other nations, and particularly the smaller nations, the opportunity to play an active role in these economic and social fields is itself a welcome opportunity in a world where political and military factors dominate the scene. It is of no small moment that the little state of Lebanon has furnished a leader in the field of human rights, or Chile a leader to the Economic and Social Council, or Thailand a leader in the field of trusteeship and dependent territories. It is not merely a matter of prestige in the ordinary political sense, it is a matter of self-respect.

Still another important by-product of international social action is the occasion it affords us to compare what we say with what we do, and to come up against what was referred to in our Declaration of Independence as "a decent respect to the opinion of mankind." It is particularly important for a nation of great power and influence to match its ideas and its conduct against the fair judgment of others, for wisdom is not necessarily an attribute of strength. A dash of humility may be a necessary ingredient of greatness as we move into the role which we are being called upon to play. It makes our task no lighter to discover that we live in the full glare of world attention and that our human frailties are magnified many times over by the criticism of our enemies or the disappointment of our friends. While we need not yield the debate to our enemies, we can acknowledge that our own job in our own society is incomplete and that we work with others as people who aspire to greater excellence than we ourselves have yet attained.

Finally, by a cooperative attack on social problems in many lands, we throw some light upon the baffling complexities of our own decisions. American foreign policy is much more than a collection of general principles enunciated periodically by authoritative spokesmen. If the things we value are to be sustained, action is required—and this action brings us into daily contact with situations of the utmost complexity in all parts of the world. Quite apart from the Cold War, we find ourselves caught between Indian and Pakistani, Jew and Arab, Dutch and Indonesian, Briton and Iranian. Sometimes our own self-interest requires us to take a hand; sometimes the parties ask us to try to find a solution; often we are importuned by one or both parties to embrace their own particular points of view; frequently we are involved by membership in an international body which is called upon to take charge of a disturbing issue. The fact remains that our role demands that we increase our knowledge and understanding of many lands and many peoples. This we cannot do quickly; sustained interest and persistent effort over extended periods of time are the price we shall have to pay for understanding. Nor will it come by the acceptance of uncritical generalities. If we are to act with a realistic appreciation of what is involved, Americans must do their learning in villages and paddy fields, in clinics and refugee camps, and not merely from statistical abstracts or the impressions of casual visitors.

Mr. Raymond B. Fosdick has reminded us of the crucial nature of the underlying moral issues of our day in the following words: "Knowledge is not enough. . . . Unless we can anchor our knowledge to moral foundations, the ultimate result will be dust and ashes. . . . The towering enemy of man is not his science but his moral inadequacy."

The true members of the emerging world community are trying to build a decent society for themselves and a more durable structure of peace. The task of building is infinitely more difficult than that of tearing down—and those outside the world community appear to be committed to tearing down what they themselves cannot control. If the material odds appear heavily against us, the odds must be reversed in the moral field. This we can try to do by seeking out common purposes and common tasks and by investing time and patience in the everyday needs of ordinary people.

Mr. Max Ascoli has said, "We work out our measure of freedom a fragment at a time." Some must work at the business of peace at the points of sharpest conflict, in the diplomatic and military fields. Others must work at the roots of conflict, by extending our horizons of knowledge and by discovering better ways of applying what we know to human needs. Those who are trained professionally for social work know how much courage and faith are needed and how stubborn are the prejudices and passions which present them with many of their central problems. It is their privilege and responsibility to help to bring our understanding and our wisdom into effective control of our strength and our technical capacity—and no profession should need a more compelling challenge.